STRESS IN TEACHING
Second Edition

The stress involved in a career in teaching has increased considerably in recent years. With the implementation of the Education Reform Act in England and Wales, a whole range of organizational and curricular changes have been added to the existing pressures of discipline problems, poor working conditions and low pay. Anxiety, depression, relationship difficulties and even physical illness are just some of the symptoms that result.

This established guide, now completely updated for teachers and managers in the 1990s, shows how to recognize the signs of stress and how to develop strategies to control it. Its practical advice, field-tested in numerous workshops for teachers and heads, will help schools to reduce pressures on their staff by the development of satisfactory whole-school policies, and teachers to be more effective in the management of their own stress levels.

Jack Dunham is a freelance stress management consultant and a tutor in Further Professional Studies at the University of Bristol. He has taught in both primary and secondary schools and worked as an educational psychologist.

STRESS IN TEACHING

Second Edition

Jack Dunham

London and New York

First published 1992
by Routledge
11 New Fetter Lane, London EC4P 4EE

Simultaneously published in the USA and Canada
by Routledge
a division of Routledge, Chapman and Hall, Inc.
29 West 35th Street, New York, NY 10001

Typeset in Palatino by Witwell Ltd, Southport
Printed and bound in Great Britain by
Biddles Ltd, Guildford and King's Lynn

British Library Cataloguing in Publication Data

A catalogue record for this title is available from the British Library.

Library of Congress Cataloging in Publication Data
Dunham, Jack.
Stress in teaching/Jack Dunham. - 2nd ed.
p.   cm.
Includes bibliographical references (p.   ) and index.
ISBN 0-415-06634-4.-ISBN 0-415-06635-2 (pbk.)
1. Teachers-Great Britain-Job Stress.   2. Teachers-Great
Britain-Workload.   I. Title.
LB2840.2.D86   1992
371.1'001'9-dc20   91-44817
                                                             CIP

For Lee and Holly
pupils in the Post Reform Era

CONTENTS

FIGURES

TABLES

PREFACE TO THE
SECOND EDITION

Since the publication of the first edition of *Stress in Teaching* in 1984 I have continued my work as a stress management consultant to schools, colleges, teachers' centres and local education authorities in the United Kingdom and the Republic of Ireland.

This work convinced me that the first edition was urgently in need of revising and updating so that my book would be as useful in the 1990s as many of you told me it was in the 1980s. The major objectives of my book are to help you identify the signs, causes and effects of the stress in teaching in the post-Reform Act era and to help you plan, prepare and implement personal and whole-school strategies for effective stress management.

A new chapter (Chapter 3) has been written to examine the effects of the seven major changes initiated by the Education Reform Act 1988. For readers outside the UK a brief outline may be helpful. The seven innovations were:

Introduction of the National Curriculum.

New requirements for religious worship.

Local management of schools.

Changes in the membership, responsibilities and powers of school governors.

Granting schools the right to opt out of local education authority control and to be funded directly (as Direct Grant Schools) from central government.

Establishment of city technology colleges funded partly from central government and partly from private donations.

Open enrolment which gives parents the right of a free choice of school for their children within the public sector.

The National Curriculum has established a statutory framework for the education of all pupils in public sector schools. There are provisions for programmes of study which are defined in the Act as 'the matters, skills and processes which are required to be taught to pupils of different abilities and maturities during each key stage. They set out the essential ground to be covered to enable pupils to meet attainment targets at the range of levels specified for each key stage.' External assessments by standardized testing are also required at each key stage, i.e. at ages 7, 11, 14 and 16. The results of the tests will be published.

The local management of Schools requires budgets to be allocated by local education authorities to each secondary school and to each primary school with more than 200 pupils. School governors have overall control in allocating resources and the day to day budgetary decisions are delegated to the headteacher and the senior management team.

These organizational and curricular changes are having a significant impact on teachers' roles and the pressures they have caused are clearly identified in Chapter 3.

All the other chapters have been reviewed and brought up to date in order to widen the applicability of the book to in-service training for headteachers, deputies, heads of department and year, teaching and non-teaching staff and for students and staff involved in initial teacher education. Modifications to the Role Conflict and Ambiguity chapter were required because of significant changes in the roles of colleagues at all levels of responsibility. Heads and deputies are becoming chief executives and business and marketing managers in addition to handling pressures from staff management. MPG (Main Professional Grade) teachers, under the demanding framework of the National Curriculum, are heavily involved in assessment as well as curriculum changes. One of my workshop members addressed these problems when he wrote that his major pressure at work is:

> The feeling that one is not doing properly something whose validity one doubts, is I'm convinced, a major cause of stress for me and my colleagues.

The chapter on Stress Reactions has also been updated to reflect the growing realization by the Education Service that occupational stress in teaching can damage the health of teachers. I also discuss the research literature and my own investigations, which indicate most strongly that stress management procedures and policies must be introduced as high priority objectives. One of my workshop members expressed the urgency of the need for action when she wrote:

> I hope that the Inset day gets moving quickly. There is no time to explore the possibility that there *might* be stress in our lives. We would do better to go in at the deep end by admitting that

teaching has become more stressful, list the things that cause stress and discuss possible solutions.

The importance of these recommendations can be readily appreciated when one learns that in the 1980s the number of teachers leaving the profession through ill health nearly trebled. Ill-health retirements in England and Wales were 1,617 in 1979 and 4,123 in 1990, with steady yearly increases in the early 1980s and a big increase in 1988. The total annual cost of stress to the Education Service has been estimated by the National Union of Teachers to be as high as £230 million.

So the final two chapters have been rewritten to include recommendations from the burgeoning stress-management literature for strengthening personal and interpersonal resources and for greatly increasing organizational resources through whole-school policies.

I have been concerned to provide more help in three areas. The first is pupil behaviour because of the strong evidence that it continues to be a major source of teacher stress. The second is teacher appraisal, which is probably going to have increasing implications for teacher stress in the 1990s both as a considerable pressure and, it is to be hoped, as a source of staff support. The third area of concern in the final chapter is that of management skills and their applications through whole-school policies for stress reduction and prevention. The chapter ends with a detailed discussion of a case study of a stress-management workshop in a sixth form college – its preparation, presentation, implementation and review – to help you in your stress-management training for staff.

I hope you enjoy reading about this workshop and the others reported in the second edition as much as I did participating in them. I am grateful to all colleagues who have contributed so readily to requests for information about their pressures, coping strategies, stress reactions and recommendations. I owe a special debt of gratitude to the sixth form college staff, for they taught me that work itself can be a coping strategy as well as a source of stress when it offers pressures which are acceptable and enjoyable. They reminded me of the 'Variety and continuing challenge of teaching'.

To enable colleagues to rediscover this experience for themselves has now become a major objective of my stress management contributions for teachers in the 1990s. I hope very much that this second edition will do this for you.

I would like to express my thanks to Vivien Bath, Mari Shullaw, Brigid Bell and Joan and Tony Walker.

ABBREVIATIONS

ACR	Annual Curriculum Return
AMMA	Assistant Masters and Mistresses Association
A/S	Advanced Supplementary
DES	Department of Education and Science
ERA	Education Reform Act
GCSE	General Certificate of Secondary Education
HMI	Her Majesty's Inspector/Inspectorate
Inset/INSET	In-service Training
LEA/lea	Local Education Authority
LMS	Local Management of Schools
MAT	Mixed Ability Teaching
MPG	Main Professional Grade
NASUWT	National Association of Schoolmasters Union of Women Teachers
NC	National Curriculum
NCC	National Curriculum Council
NFER	National Foundation for Educational Research
PCAS	Polytechnics Central Admissions System
PGCE	Post Graduate Certificate of Education
ROA	Record of Achievement
RSA	Royal Society of Arts
TES	Times Educational Supplement
UCCA	Universities Central Council for Admissions

1

INTRODUCTION

The first step in tackling stress is to acknowledge its existence in teaching. Acceptance is difficult for people who associate stress with personal weakness and professional incompetence. For them, admitting to classroom difficulties is tantamount to admitting that they are bad teachers. They are afraid to disclose professional problems to colleagues who would regard them as signs of failure. They are unwilling to ask for help because that action would be seen as a form of weakness. Some of these barriers to stress reduction were identified by a teacher in a report sent to me in preparation for a staff conference: 'Stress is caused because I am unable to ask for extra support because if I did, I would be assessed as as weak teacher by the rest of the staff.'

The second step is to be clear about what the term 'stress' means, because several definitions are used by teachers. This issue of meaning is important because we need to know which definition teachers are using when they accept or deny the existence of stress.

There are three major approaches to understanding the nature of stress in teaching. The first approach looks at the pressure exerted on teachers in schools. A parallel is drawn with Hooke's Law of Electricity, the main elements of which are that of 'stress' (the load or demand which is placed on metal) and that of 'strain' (the deformation that results). The law states that if the strain produced by a given stress falls within the 'elastic limit' of the material, then when the stress is removed the material will simply return to its original condition. If, however, the strain passes beyond the 'elastic limit', then some permanent damage will result. This model suggests that people, too, have their limits. Up to a point, stress can be tolerated, but when it becomes intolerable, damage may result, either psychological or physiological, or both. From this perspective stress 'is a set of causes, not a set of symptoms' (Symonds 1947: 1). This is still a widely held view and it is the basis of the argument that only certain groups of teachers, for example probationers, need programmes of guidance and support. This engineering model, equating external pressures with stress, can be criticized on a number of grounds. There are wide individual differences among teachers in their reactions to their first year of service, reorganization, redeployment or other pressures. Some of them report stimulation rather than stress during these experiences. The extent to which the work demands made upon a teacher result in stress depends on a number of factors including pressures from sources external to teaching: personality and previous experience of similar demands.

The second approach to understanding stress is concerned with the forms taken by teachers' reactions to these pressures. These may consist of emotional and bodily manifestations such as headaches, muscular tension and stomach ailments. From this perspective stress is defined as 'an unpleasant emotional state (e.g. tension, frustration, anxiety, emotional exhaustion)' (Kyriacou 1981: 193). This view defines the concept of stress in terms of the degree to which a person is experiencing persistent and high levels of anxiety or tension, identified in symptoms such as 'agitated', 'depressed', 'irritable', 'weepy', 'like a wet rag', 'can't concentrate', 'very tense' and 'can't switch off'. This perspective is illustrated in a letter I received from a member of one of my Further Professional Studies courses in Bristol University's School of Education:

> I should like to ask you a few questions concerning a friend of mine who has been teaching in a comprehensive school for four years. At the same time she has had fairly massive domestic problems. Since the second week of term she has been on sick leave. Her symptoms are persistent nausea, bouts of panic with very rapid heartbeats, sleeplessness, terrible feelings of panic and a tingling sensation in her limbs. Her doctor is treating her for stress but what I really wanted to ask you was:
>
> 1 Are these typical symptoms of stress?
> 2 How long do they take to be cured?
> 3 Does the cure involve leaving the teaching profession?
> 4 Are the symptoms, if cured for the moment, likely to recur?

These questions bring out the strong medical orientation of this approach to understanding stress which is one of its major weaknesses. There are important manifestations which are not emotional or psychosomatic and so tend to be ignored by people using this definition. A head of department expressed one difficulty during an in-service training course: 'The awareness of stress is an important issue. Many people seem unable to recognize the signs in themselves or feel that they are letting themselves down if they admit to stress.'

One significant type of problem which is frequently not defined as stress-related is ineffectiveness in the performance of one's role in school. The experience of becoming ineffective is often accompanied by a major loss of confidence and is particularly worrying to staff who have been competent and confident for a number of years. Some of the consequences of a reduction in effort and competence because of an increase in stress were set out very clearly by a head of department in a preparatory report to me for a stress reduction workshop:

> I tried hard to forget school during the vacation and I refused for the first time in ten years to spend time in the classroom before the holiday was over. I did not finish my aims and objectives for which the head had been waiting. I tried to accept that my time and talent were limited but I find it very hard. I have used more available and less original material in my lessons. For the first time I have re-issued notes from previous years.

The third approach to explaining stress is concerned with both pressures and reactions and also with the coping resources which teachers use as they attempt to cope with their difficulties. Stress from this perspective means a significant excess of pressures over coping resources. This interactionist approach emphasizes the importance of identifying the demands which teachers perceive and experience as stressful and the behaviour they use to tackle these demands. Coping behaviour has been defined by Mechanic (1967) as the application of a person's acquired skills, techniques and knowledge and he has argued that, in attempting to understand stress, more attention should be given to problem-solving and coping behaviour.

This view proposes that the extent to which a teacher experiences stress in any situation in school depends upon a number of factors which include: appraisal of demands and his or her strategies to deal with them; anticipation of likely future demanding experiences and his or her state of readiness to tackle them; the extent of the preparation and rehearsal of the skills necessary for the teacher to handle work pressures effectively.

I use the interactionist model as the basis of my in-service training in stress reduction skills and it will be used as the framework for this book. My definition of stress is: a process of behavioural, emotional, mental, and physical reactions caused by prolonged, increasing or new pressures which are significantly greater than coping resources. The plan of the book follows the three parts of the definition (pressures, reactions and coping resources): Chapters 2, 3 (the additional chapter), 4, 5, and 6 are concerned with helping teachers in primary and secondary schools to become more aware of the pressures which are experienced by their colleagues so that they can be encouraged to identify their own pressures. Chapter 7 is related to the demands on headteachers and deputy heads and chapter 8 discusses the heavy loads experienced by heads of departments, heads of houses and year heads; chapter 9 reports the stress reactions of all staff and chapter 10 records the different strategies which staff use as they tackle their pressures and reactions. In chapters 11 and 12 I offer a number of recommendations for strengthening coping resources.

These chapters use information which has been reported by staff in my action research projects in courses and conferences in schools, colleges, teachers' centres and universities. The research is an integral part of the awareness and skills training. Before a course or conference begins, I ask for information about the members' pressures, reactions, resources and recommendations for the reduction of stress. This is summarized and reported back when I participate in the session. If it is a school-based staff conference, I visit the school and interview some of the staff before the conference, and then while it is in progress I report back my information and also suggest a framework for a stress-reduction programme for staff. Reporting back is an essential test for the accuracy of my perception of how staff are dealing with the sources of stress in school. A follow-up session to review the effectiveness of the stress-reduction programme after about six months is gradually becoming more accepted by teachers as a necessary part of my work.

For the first edition in 1984 I collected written and oral information from about 1,350 teachers, including heads, deputies, heads of departments and house and year heads, and from another 4,190 staff between then and the middle of 1991. Much of it is presented in this book, which I see as another form of feed-back to be tested for its accuracy by teachers individually and in groups. A considerable amount of information is presented in the words of the teachers themselves so that their collegues can share these experiences of stress, learn from their attempts to reduce it and, perhaps most importantly, end their feelings of suffering from stress in isolation. In this book, as in my in-service training, I see myself as a facilitator and not as an 'expert' and I offer it with thanks to all my respondents who have helped me so much personally and professionally.

2

PROBLEMS CAUSED BY ORGANIZATIONAL AND CURRICULAR CHANGES BEFORE THE REFORM ACT 1988

In this chapter there is an investigation of the major changes teachers experienced in the decade before the Reform Act and which altered their schools and the work they did in the classrooms. These included the demands of reorganization and the development of schemes of pastoral care for pupils with personal and family problems. Staff were also under pressure to use new and more rigorous methods for appraisal of their work and to maintain high professional standards in the face of reduced financial support in schools.

For the majority of teachers, reorganization originally meant the organizational and curricular changes which were required to implement their LEA's policy for comprehensive education. This earlier reorganization was associated with growth and was very different from contemporary developments, which are usually based on contraction. For some teachers the establishment of comprehensive schools had a very positive meaning. They felt, as one of the teachers expressed it to me: 'A sense of relief and a sense of not being bottled up, even of liberation'. These teachers perceived new opportunities for fresh patterns of teaching; new relationships; new patterns of involvement in worthwhile developments; fresh opportunities for personal and professional growth and better prospects for promotion. But for some of their colleagues the process of moving from a secondary modern or grammar school into a comprehensive school meant changes which seemed to have four major aspects:

1 leaving the security of a familiar environment in the previous school;
2 working in larger and more complex schools;
3 teaching pupils who had a much wider range of abilities, behaviour and attitudes;
4 adapting to major organizational and curricular changes.

Some of these changes were perceived before reorganization as threats and viewed with apprehension. During my discussions with teachers about the adjustments they would have to make to achieve a successful transition to the comprehensive systems in their LEA, a number of worries were expressed. Staff were concerned about the differences between their present pupils and those in the new school. They were apprehensive about the problems of discipline they might encounter. They thought that they would have to modify their own patterns of behaviour to which they had become accustomed over a number of years. These familiar routines and rituals had given them security because there were so few unexpected demands. Unfortunately the limitations of a narrow range of school experience made them vulnerable to the uprooting aspect of reorganization.

The significance of this kind of vulnerability can be seen in the experience of a teacher who had been working in a new purpose-built comprehensive school for about a year. She told me that she was experiencing much less job satisfaction in her present school than in the small country grammar school which had been her only post and in which she had worked for ten years. Reorganization had brought several losses: she and her colleagues were required to leave the old grammar school buildings and to move into new buildings on a new site. She also left behind her headmaster who chose the time of reorganization to retire. He had ruled the school as a benevolent and autocratic father-figure for over twenty years. The man appointed to take his place seemed inadequate to her because he was not satisfying her needs for recognition and support. She said she was depressed. She seemed to be suffering from grief for the loss of the grammar school and of the kind of working life it had meant for her.

But reorganization meant more than trying to come to terms with personal losses. It was necessary for staff to attempt to cope with the differences in the new school. For many teachers this meant working in a much larger school and for them this was one of the most severe demands they encountered. The process of adaptation to a larger school has been perceptively analysed by the head of an Avon secondary school (Hinton 1974: 17): 'Most of us are simply unused to very large schools. We went to smaller schools; we taught in smaller schools. It is a slow and uneasy process adjusting to a different kind of institution.'

One of the important differences he identified was the difficulty of developing a sense of belonging to a big organization. In the largest schools there was a considerable risk that the organization would be perceived as so impersonal and so fragmented that a sense of common purpose would be very difficult to achieve. In these circumstances it became difficult to find points of identification with staff and pupils. For teachers who had served in small schools where they felt the satisfaction of shared aims, the demands involved in these changes presented severe problems. These large schools were also much more complex organizations which included split-site working, complicated disciplinary procedures, impersonal communication systems instead of the face-to-face contact of previous schools and new administrative structures which included executive teams, policy and planning committees and staff working parties.

Teachers going into comprehensive schools were also required to adjust to a different intake of pupils with a much wider range of behaviour, abilities and attitudes. A minority of these pupils had learning, disciplinary and emotional problems which were outside the training and experience of their teachers. Some long-serving members of staff with the limited experience which made them vulnerable to change had a demoralizing awareness of incompetence and loss of confidence for the first time for many years. They were surprised and occasionally shocked at the behaviour and language of their pupils. One teacher reported: 'It is not the physical aspects which cause difficulty, as these are not too extreme, so much as the psychological battering one receives to one's ego; for example one's requests being ignored and the verbal abuse.'

These teachers were also disturbed by the intensity of their own emotional reactions in classroom, corridor and staff-room. Their previous teaching had not aroused their emotions so strongly: they had simulated anger for disciplinary purposes – now they were really angry; they believed that teaching was like playing a dramatic role on the stage – now their own attitudes, values and skills were being tested to the full.

The demands made on the staff were compounded in a number of schools by major organizational and curricular changes. These pressures have been clearly identified by the head of the Avon secondary school I quoted earlier in this chapter:

> When schools go comprehensive teachers are thrust into a variety
> of quite unfamiliar teaching and pastoral situations. They have to
> cope with children of both sexes, all ages and abilities, with a
> plethora of new methods and curricula and with changing atti-
> tudes and standards which often seem to devalue skills and
> philosophies in which they have a heavy emotional investment.
> They have to adjust to a large number of new colleagues in the
> immediate aftermath of the anxiety and disturbance which
> reorganization inevitably brings.

The possible sources of stress which the head has identified were not staggered to give teachers the opportunity of adjusting to one major change before having to cope with the next one. In the schools where all the problems associated with secondary school reorganization were experienced by staff almost simultaneously, resistance to present and further changes became a self-protective strategy. It was clearly expressed in a staff report which was discussed at a secondary-school staff-development conference in which I participated:

> We felt that when this school was opened we were thrown into far too much change. There were too many ideas that we were trying to operate all at the same time and this gave us a great deal of insecurity. We lacked stability. We had far too many things that we could not cope with and this was the root cause of our trouble. We felt that it was not too late to impose some stability, to stop the changes, to keep going as we are and build slowly on what we have got. We want to improve the quality of life for the children in the school but we cannot do this when we are developing too rapidly to give ourselves a secure base from which to work.

One of the early innovations in this school, as in other comprehensive schools, was mixed-ability teaching. When I visited the school to interview staff and prepare for their staff development conference it was apparent that a considerable number of teachers were experiencing difficulties as a consequence of teaching unstreamed classes of pupils with very different attainments in the basic subjects. The headteacher had circulated a questionnaire to assess their opinions about teaching attainment groups. In their replies staff indicated their feelings of worry and inadequacy. One teacher wrote:

> I lack personal experience of MAT as I do not teach the first and second years but the casual comments of my colleagues are discouraging. I am very worried at the dilution of the academic content of the school and the bland assumption that mixing will somehow raise the morale of the less able but not work conversely with the more able.

One of her colleagues expressed her feelings much more briefly: 'I am not qualified nor able to cope with MA teaching.'

Similar pressures on teachers arising from the change to working with unstreamed groups have been reported by other writers, one of whom concluded after a major study of organizational and curricular changes in a comprehensive school: 'Once the problem of looking critically at teaching methods is faced, teachers find themselves having to embark on the painful process of reassessing their own skills, perhaps after years of successful teaching' (Richardson 1973: 334).

Pressures arising from the many different kinds of changes involved in secondary-school reorganization have not ended. There are schemes being submitted to the Secretary of State and decisions are being taken about them which will have major consequences for the teachers concerned. Details of this kind of problem were given to me by the deputy head of a grammar school:

The problem I am likely to be faced with in the near future is concerned with secondary reorganization. This has been impending for the last twenty years but a decision seems possible later this year. The scheme before the Secretary of State involves converting this school into a Sixth Form College. The problem for the staff will be that although all of them with a couple of exceptions want to be in the Sixth Form College it is not likely than more than 50 per cent will be. However the reorganization proposals require all the staff, whether they have a future in the Sixth Form College or not, to work in the dwindling Grammar School during the interim period of around four years. Early retirement will not be an option as we have virtually no staff over 45 and their chances of being employed in other similar schools to ours are naturally very limited. A new Head starts next term. How do I minimalize the stress and loss of morale of those staff who do not get jobs in the Sixth Form College but have to stay in the Grammar School for as long as it exists? I suppose it's a common problem but not one that is in my experience.

Another secondary school in the same LEA is also facing major changes which were identified by the head in a letter inviting me to take part in a staff in-service training day:

This school is a three-form entry girls' secondary modern school. At present the role stands at 500 but this will soon drop to approximately 465. There are thirty members of staff including myself. I believe that my staff, in common with those in other schools, are under considerable pressures at the moment with falling rolls and the prospect of reorganization of the city schools in a year's time. I shall be grateful therefore if you can air this problem and give us some guidance in coping with it as a staff.

The reorganization which these teachers will encounter very shortly will be a merger with another secondary school in the city. This will create several changes for the staff of both schools, but one of the most important will be alterations in the roles of those teachers with management responsibilities: headteachers, deputies, heads of department and heads of houses and years. It is highly unlikely that job-sharing will be introduced by this LEA. What is much more probable is that there will be a reduction in the status, prestige and job satisfaction for those members of staff not appointed to their previous levels of responsibility in the new school. An indication of the possible effects of these changes was contained in a letter sent to me by a head of department shortly before one of my courses for middle management. He wrote:

My main source of stress in my present post has been brought about by the following situation – I am head of a department in a 'new' school brought about by a merger. In the department there are also two other teachers who have been head of department in the 'old' school which now houses the new school. It has been difficult on occasions to introduce new ideas and changes without causing upset and I have been extremely aware of the anxiety and stress for all concerned. I have tried to overcome certain situations by taking on jobs myself and therefore lessening the stress situation. Making decisions without consultation with others has helped as it lessens any conflict situation which we all politely try to avoid. Sometimes I switch off completely and adopt an action which takes me right away from it all – playing squash is one way for me.

The teachers in this school who were not appointed to the head of department positions are also being affected by another major change. Earlier in their careers if this problem had occurred they would have sought and probably obtained a similar post or gained promotion in another school. But at the present time these opportunities are more restricted and they are likely to feel that further promotion either inside or outside the school is improbable. This has resulted in some instances of the development of feelings of being 'trapped'. The problem is not restricted to heads of department and an indication of the meaning of contraction for other teachers is contained in the report of a deputy head:

> Large numbers of teachers are unable to gain further promotion. This in itself has led to a certain discontentment among staff, which affects their relations with the hierarchy, but add this to the fact that discretionary posts are not being refilled when they fall vacant (due to educational cuts) and you have a worsening situation in which the work-load of Third Deputies and Senior Teachers may well be shared among teachers who already feel frustrated at their inability to gain promotion.

This major change from expansion to contraction in the Education Service as a whole and in the career prospects of teachers has also been strongly felt in primary schools, where the growth of urgent financial problems is accelerating. The cuts in educational expenditure are producing a continually changing pattern of economies which impose serious pressures. These include reductions in staffing at all levels; a virtually complete embargo on all appointments – even of replacements; the restriction of building repairs and maintenance; reductions in support provision such as the School Psychological Service and the

Remedial Education Service; capitation allowances frozen at a fraction of the previous year's allowance and reductions in meal-time staffing.

Some of the increasing pressures on the heads and teachers in the primary schools of one LEA arising from these cuts, were reported by the headteachers:

1 Reduction in part-time teaching staff, so headteachers have more teaching time.
2 Reduction in secretarial hours, so heads have less help to deal with administration (which is increasing).
3 Reduction in school meals allowances, so that meals sent to school leave no room for flexibility, which results in stress to school meals staff and the head.
4 Total cut of remedial assistance, which means that the staff have to give a lot more time to certain children at the expense of others.
5 Teachers have to spend more hours in school talking, preparing, etc.
6 Teachers have to make do with limited resources and so share books between children or do group work because of it. The class organization and curriculum are governed by the available resources, not what the teacher thinks is the best method of working.
7 Less mobility in the teaching profession means there are fewer opportunities for promotion.

Two other important problems have been identified. They are staff allocation and redeployment. The possible sources of stress in each of these situations have been clearly presented by a head in another LEA. For the last five years his school has suffered falling rolls, which together with the cuts in public spending has led to a reduced staffing allocation for the school. He was invited by his Education Officer to make out a case for extra staff for 'curriculum support'. The head also arranged to hold special meetings of governors and parents and petitions and letters were sent to Councillors and the Education Committee to back up his requests for extra staff. The sources of stress in this situation for the head were:

1 The 'here we go again' feeling. There was resentment at the time and effort involved in struggling to retain the status quo rather than working to improve things. A slow erosion of morale resulted from this for all the staff.
2 Anxiety over what would happen if there were no 'reprieve' because it was emphasized by the Education Officer at a governors' meeting that there would be no reprieve this time. This would have meant classes of up to 35 in small classrooms and would have drastically undermined the basis of the school with its emphasis on the development of the individual child. [There was a reprieve.]

3 The time and effort involved in writing reports, collecting information about details of special needs, etc., holding meetings with
governors and parents, writing letters to Councillors.
4 Poor relationships with the Education Office personnel. The
uncertainty seemed to lead to a sort of paranoia when nobody was
trusted.

The redeployment problem for this head occurred in the summer term,
when the Education Officer decided to advertise for only two of three
vacancies and to leave the third open for the possible redeployment of a
teacher. The decision was taken after the final date for serving teachers
to give notice of resignation, so the applications were restricted to
probationers and temporary staff (over 300 applied). Two teachers
were appointed. A teacher who had been nominated for redeployment
was sent to the school to be interviewed for the third vacancy. She was
well qualified; she had also recently changed schools twice. After
meeting her the head and the staff decided they could not accept her as
a colleague. The teacher was 'passed on' to another school. It was now
near the end of the summer term and to the head it seemed like a 'war
of nerves' between the Education Office administrators and the school.
Finally two weeks before the end of term, the Education Officer told
the head that he could appoint the teacher of his choice. One of the
shortlisted applicants for the two other posts was still available and was
appointed.

The head did not learn much about the feelings of the redeployed
teacher who was not appointed. He said she shared his embarrassment.
There is a possibility of more serious consequences for redeployed
teachers, some of which can be noted in my interview with a teacher in
an infants school. She contacted me shortly after the end of the
summer term. I went to interview her at her home and I asked her to
write a record of the major events of the last two weeks of term. Her
report starts with the staff being told that the school had to lose one
teacher:

Friday 6th July
There was a Staff Meeting to discuss the redeployment of a
teacher. Our Adviser came to tell us, the whole staff both Junior
and Infant teachers, that at the end of term one of the full-time
teachers would have to go. After a general discussion with vague
facts and points raised by only a few of the staff, i.e. the deputy
head, the head of infants, myself and one other, we were invited
to have individual interviews with the Adviser, the headmaster
also being present. Half of the staff stayed on for these interviews
(it being 5.30) and the rest were to have interviews on Monday. I
had my interview on Friday. Three main questions were asked:

age, mobility, dependants. Various other points may have been raised. The interview was fairly relaxed, but one felt almost fatalistic about it. (All the staff came out of the interview feeling it was going to be them!)

Monday 9 July
We all knew the Adviser was coming; there was therefore obvious concern which appeared to be felt by everyone and his possible arrival was a constant topic of conversation. He must have arrived in the middle of the afternoon because at 3.20 I was summoned by the Headmaster to see him again. There was a sinking feeling and an instant realization that it was going to be me! The interview was even in the same room as the interviews for redeployment held in 1977. The Adviser told me immediately that he was asking me to be redeployed. My immediate reaction was '*Why me?*' He hummed and haa'd for a bit and then said I was experienced and I was possibly the 'best' one, i.e. adaptable. I cannot remember the exact words. I was naturally upset but able to cope with the situation. As the headmaster was not present, I felt able to talk openly, and I mentioned tactfully and briefly that I had been almost redeployed before. I wanted to find out if possible if the headmaster had been involved in the choice. The Adviser said not, and I suppose I wanted to agree with him – he had been seen to be very fair – and was now being very understanding and as helpful as possible in the circumstances. After a long discussion we then went into the headmaster's office. I did go into the staffroom briefly – to find the deputy head and a junior teacher who had waited behind to see me. The rest of the staff had gone home previously. The Adviser was obviously anxious to go – he said he had to go and see a junior headmaster. Did I want to go with him? A junior post? Certainly not, I said – I am a fully qualified and experienced infant teacher. The headmaster gave me a lift home. Then followed a night of telephone calls and no sleep (I dropped off between 3 and 5), waking early, exhausted and *very* agitated and concerned. During the night my main feeling was one of intense anger and frustration and panic.

Friday 20th July
My last teaching day at the school was spent clearing up, completing some records and organizing my own boxes of equipment. The lunch time celebrations in the staffroom proved to be quite light-hearted (there were three teachers leaving) and I had a sad and very touching farewell from my children and especially my parents. Those I know well came in to give me a beautiful present – a bouquet – and make their goodbyes.

13

Monday 23rd July
I went into school to complete my packing and leave my boxes in the corridor. The infant teacher who was taking over my room, together with the Head of Infants, was in the process of dismantling the shelf areas and completely changing the whole room. I must admit I felt as though it was an acknowledgement of how little I had achieved. I know it wasn't, but it did leave me feeling rather lost and inadequate.

Wednesday 25th July
Now I have to do all my records of attainment, etc., in the holidays. Unfortunately I always like to do them thoroughly and before the end of term – usually in the last two weeks. But this has been no ordinary end of term for me. The records will be done in the holiday as thoroughly as the circumstances will permit. Half of me feels why should I bother? But that is not the way I work and I will attempt to do the work to the best of my ability, e.g. the social/emotional records, the attainment records of Maths and Reading/Writing (all personal to the school) and the new Mathematics and Literacy Records, of which the latter require the presence of the children. But as I said before this is not an ordinary end of term, or for that matter, the usual beginning to the summer holiday.

The effect of redeployment on the school as a whole should also be considered, because the pressures may affect more people than is at first apparent. This was the firm conclusion of the deputy head of a secondary school who presented several important issues in her report:

We have experienced serious problems when going through the redeployment procedure. They are:
1 The effects on the identified staff, which are mainly emotional and traumatic and which are reflected on to their families. They feel they have been rejected by their school; they feel that they are no good and that they have no future in the profession.
2 The effects on the colleagues of the identified staff in the staffroom, which appear to be mainly feelings of guilt and uncertainty about how to react.
3 The relationships between the identified staff and senior colleagues have become very fragile and in some cases they have been destroyed.
4 The role of the LEA staff is very important. They should not consult with the headteacher and the deputies in identifying the member of staff and then withdraw, leaving the school to pick up the pieces; this is most important for it is not sufficient just

to encourage the teacher to apply for suitable jobs – they require much more guidance.

5 The role of union representative can be very tricky, but representatives have a crucial part to play.

The leaving part of the redeployment process which is discussed in my interview and in this report may not be the most difficult part of these changes. Adjusting to a new school in these circumstances can bring heavy pressures. This appeared to be the experience of five redeployed teachers who talked about some of their problems:

I felt that the head had been forced to accept me.
I felt that I had been forced to accept the job.
I felt that my colleagues regarded me with suspicion.
I think the head resents having to appoint me.
I think a redeployed teacher is a kind of stigma.

These five teachers had been redeployed because their school was closing at the end of the school year. School closures will continue to put a number of teachers 'at risk' in relation to stress, but there are probably more staff experiencing heavy demands because of the *threat* of school closure. Some of these pressures were identified by the head of a primary school whose school had been visited by the County Council Falling Rolls Panel in the previous year. After this visit the Panel proposed that his school should be closed as part of a reorganization plan for the area. The stress caused by this proposal was considerable for everyone in the school, and at my invitation the head analysed the stress situations which he had experienced:

1 Extra paper work: Obviously I am heavily committed to the opposition of these proposals and this has involved me in a considerable amount of extra paper work which includes:
(a) Preparation of school dossier.
(b) Research and preparation of a document which gave the arguments for the survival of the school.
(c) Increase in Report to Governors (average of three Governors meetings per term). This, in a way, has been a good exercise in that it helps one reappraise one's values and principles in education.

2 Press/TV/Radio: Both local and national press and TV (plus Schools Radio) have taken an interest in our case and this has led to a considerable amount of time and 'stress energy' being spent on press interviews, etc.

3 'Spreading the Word': I have found it particularly stressful to repeat the arguments of our case over and over again to a variety of people in all walks of life. It is important to do this to gain the

support we need, but changing one's language style to suit the type of listener (i.e. not being too technical to the non-professional, yet presenting a clear and reasoned argument) is a type of stress that seems unnoticeable at first, but would appear to have a cumulative effect as time goes on.

4 The Parents: Although I have enjoyed considerable support from the parents, and this is a valuable resource, it has been paid for with a lot of diplomacy! This includes taking time to talk to individuals, making sure they are kept informed of developments and organizing meetings in the evenings.

5 Governors: Again, these have been a source of support, but the extra liaison needed over the fight to save the school has caused extra worry and time consumption.

6 Time: All these demands involve spending a lot of time on extra work. As a 'teaching head' this has meant less time with my family and although they understand the problems and have given me a lot of support it has caused tension at home.

7 The stress factor has been considerable during the past year because of the proposals which were added to the normal pressures of everyday teaching.

The ordinary demands of primary-school teaching, to which this head refers, have also increased in recent years. They include team teaching; the use of modern teaching methods which emphasize the importance of individual children's needs; the rapid expansion of the curriculum to include science, drama, new forms of craft, dance, 'new' mathematics and computers; the expansion of out-of-school activities; the requirements of new legislation, fêtes, competitions and sales to raise funds for the school. These changes in primary and secondary schools were not properly assimilated and I suggested in the first edition a moratorium of 5 years to give teachers the opportunity to come to terms with recent and current innovations in their schools. In this period, instead of a halt or slowing down for assimilation, there have been unprecedented changes at a relentless rate to the teacher's role.

These pressures included TVEI and TVEE, Records of Achievement, IT, GCSE courses, Industrial Action and Required Time. Some of these initiatives, such as GCSE courses with continuous assessment deadlines, Records of Achievement and IT, brought drastic curricular and organizational changes. The implementation of these developments required the use of different teaching and learning styles for which most teachers had not been trained.

The teachers' industrial action in the mid-1980s brought marked alterations to attitudes and activities, to communications between management and staff and to the leadership styles of headteachers. It also marked the beginning of a movement away from a professional role perspective to an employee orientation which, as I shall argue in the next chapter, is still affecting teachers' motivation.

Extra-curricular activities and some school-based responsibilities were curtailed, giving teachers the opportunity to reflect on the benefits to them of these restrictions. But some teachers had parallel feelings of guilt for 'letting the pupils down'. A teacher in a comprehensive school expressed this dilemma to me quite clearly:

> I feel that I have been unable to provide the advice/guidance which is normally available to pupils *re* careers. They are missing out and any guidance given at other times is very rushed. On the personal side, leaving school at lunchtime does provide a pleasant break from the routine of school and in some respects I feel more refreshed for the afternoon sessions.

More negative and positive reactions were reported to me. The negative ones included an increase in behavioural problems and vandalism at lunchtimes and afternoon lessons. A deputy head articulated these problems in considerable detail:

> As a deputy covering the school at lunchtime I am exhausted by trying to retain standards without the assistance of other colleagues. Obtaining supply staff has totally taken over my daily activities and arranging class cover with regard to different union affiliations increases the complexity. The atmosphere in school has suffered, disciplinary standards have weakened, it is less easy to teach in the afternoons, the ethos gained from extra-curricular activity is disappearing fast and is reflected in pupils' attitudes in the classroom as well as around the building. My own teaching has suffered greatly, administration is less efficient, forward planning minimal and illness amongst colleagues does not appear to be diminishing in the slightest. I have yet to note a single benefit and feel extremely frustrated, overstressed and look forward to early retirement a.s.a.p.

But several important positive aspects were put forward by teachers in my workshops. These included:

1 Increased self-esteem – belief in doing something positive to change a situation. Acting on longheld principles and beliefs to improve the quality of education.
2 Increased morale.
3 Group strength.
4 In-service training for many – learning to speak at meetings, produce

pamphlets, relate to parents, negotiate with senior staff – people in my school have greatly increased in confidence and competence.

5 Increased contacts with other teachers locally and nationally – developing and expanding support systems.

I compiled the statements made in my workshops into a questionnaire which was completed by 110 teachers in comprehensive schools (see Appendix, p.187). The statements of positive and negative reactions with the largest number of responses were:

- Mine are positive because of opportunities of relaxation at lunchtime (62 per cent).
- I am frustrated because I think that relationships and communication with parents will not be re-established for a long time (61 per cent).
- Mine are positive because of guaranteed non-teaching time for preparation, marking or even relaxing (59 per cent).
- Leaving school at lunchtime does provide a pleasant break from the routine of school (55 per cent).
- I am worried by possible 'parental negativity' to the action taken by the staff (54 per cent).
- My reactions are negative because of my colleagues' growing dis-illusionment with the job, e.g. two departmental heads are leaving teaching without having a job to go to (53 per cent).
- Mine are negative because of the conflict between those who have acted and those who have not (44 per cent).
- My feelings are negative as the parents and children in my school seem to be developing the idea that teachers are a non-caring group (44 per cent).
- My reactions are positive because unnecessary meetings are a thing of the past (40 per cent).
- My feelings about industrial action are negative because vandalism and bad behaviour have increased (40 per cent).

This mixed group of reactions from secondary school teachers provides a very interesting comparison with the results from four workshops of headteachers of primary schools totalling ninety members. Their percentage responses were:

- Mine are negative because industrial action has increased the pressures on the headteacher (56 per cent).
- My feelings are negative because new teachers and students on teaching practice will take the current situation to be the norm (43 per cent).
- I am frustrated because very little is happening within the depart-ment (38 per cent).

- Mine are negative because industrial action might kill extra-curricular activities (37 per cent).
- I am worried by possible 'parental negativity' to the action taken by staff (36 per cent).
- Industrial action has brought the negative result of a lessening of communication between management and staff, e.g. now only by printed messages (35 per cent).
- Mine are negative because of conflict between those who have acted and those who have not (33 per cent).
- My feelings are negative as the parents and children in my school seem to be developing the idea that teachers are a non-caring group (33 per cent).
- My reactions are negative because of my colleagues' growing disillusionment with the job, e.g. two departmental heads are leaving teaching without having a job to go to (31 per cent).

Mixed reactions amongst teachers to directed time have also been reported. Some teachers saw advantages: better management of meetings, forward planning, communication with colleagues and time were most frequently noted in a survey by Cowan and Wright (1989), who also found, however, that the most commonly listed disadvantages were erosion of extra-curricular activities, encouraging clock-watching, creating resentment, irrelevant meetings, destroying goodwill and staff morale and diminishing the professsional status of teachers.

The imposition of the contract of 1,265 hours in the aftermath of the industrial action of the 1980s appeared to result in significant reactions. Cowan and Wright found them to be:

Staff feel resentful, depressed and devalued
There is a considerable rise in the levels of stress experienced by teachers and heads.
Frustration is caused by an increase in meetings and administration.
Staff are not so co-operative.

One respondent's comment was used by the investigation to sum up the views of many respondents:

And you feel so bloody insulted that the DES is telling you you're lazy and need to be tied to 1,265 hours.

The research workers sum up their own experience in this project by claiming that it has produced evidence of the 'current dissatisfaction and frustration of our teaching force'. They warn that:

Coping with the demands of the National Curriculum, the Education Reform Act, Local Management of Schools, not to mention

staffing shortages will necessitate staff resorting to unprecedented personal resources in order to survive.

(Cowan and Wright 1989: 388)

These initiatives and their effects on teachers are discussed in the next
chapter.

3

THE EFFECTS OF THE REFORM ACT 1988 ON TEACHERS' ROLES

The Reform Act provided the biggest package of initiatives in the 1980s and arguably 'the biggest single change in education this century' (Wragg 1990). Some details of these developments were given by the headteacher of a primary school who was a member of one of my recent stress management workshops. She wrote:

> The major pressures are the increasing complexity and accountability of the job, e.g. coping with the Local Management of Schools, the National Curriculum, etc. There is a lack of time for planning and discussion in order to prepare for their implementation. There is the additional pressure of formulating an Institutional Development Plan by the end of this term. I see this as a large undertaking especially as the English curriculum document has not arrived for consultation yet.

This headteacher also reported marked changes in parents' and children's attitudes. She said that they need an increasing amount of counselling and support. But she also found that parents are challenging the rules of the school more frequently, for example harrassing teachers in the classroom during teaching time.

Another headteacher in the same workshop told us that she was having to demand more and more from the staff to implement the National Curriculum on time. The teachers have no time free from a class even though some of them have additional management and consultant's responsibilities.

Teachers in comprehensive schools are also meeting the challenge of Open Enrolment, the Local Management of Schools, the National Curriculum and the Institute Development Plan. They have also had to find the time and energy to manage the introduction of GCSE courses. One teacher on another recent stress management workshop told me:

21

We have just begun GCSE courses, therefore there is much planning and lots of assessments (Science) required. We have assessments on all the students every six weeks and parents' consultations with 75 per cent attendance. There is high pupil and management expectation. They expect things to happen fast!

For some teachers the introduction of GCSE courses has meant that radical alterations to their role have been needed. The essential requirements of project work and very regular assessment involve new methods of working for many members of staff. These innovations have resulted in increased paperwork, meetings and moderations of assessments.

These changes were preceded by others which considerably altered another aspect of teachers' roles. The changes in salary structure brought changes in the allocation of promoted posts. These changes particularly affected those members of staff who previously held Scale 2 posts. They perceived themselves to have gone backwards in their careers. This view has been reinforced by the sharp reduction in promotion opportunities which has been experienced by many teachers. So, instead of an expanding and developing role many colleagues feel that they are trapped in a contracting Education Service.

Some teachers in secondary schools have had their perception of what their roles involve challenged even more by feeling under considerable pressure from several sources, including the Government, parents, school governors, the media, industry and Local Education Authorities, to establish strong links with local employers. These recommendations are perceived as strong indicators that the predominant values which should guide teachers' performance of their roles are those of market-place economics, that is cost-effectiveness, cost-cutting, profit and increased efficiency. The predominant theme is value for money.

These demands have been identified for secondary school teachers and for some of their colleagues in primary schools by preparation for the implementation of Local Management of Schools. The balance sheet and the bursar are awarded increasing recognition and some school activities reduced because of many demands for a share of the budget. This initiative carries the main thrust of the Government's privatization policy. Its beliefs, values and language are very different from those held by many serving teachers and they present a culture shock which is as severe as it is sudden. This was epitomized for me by an infant school teacher when she gave me her meaning of LMS: 'we can now be sacked'.

This teacher's premonition of radical alterations in some teachers' working lives has been borne out by reported events in the first year of the new decade. These reports of enforced redundancies have included:

A Wiltshire History teacher is the first teacher to face compulsory redundancy because of legislation to give hire and fire power to heads and governors of schools – surplus to its needs.

(Gow 1989: 6)

Mrs Symes, a teacher at Redlands Church of England First School in Dorking, Surrey for twelve years, is being made redundant by the school governors following the change to local management under the Education Reform Act.

(Knewstub 1990: 6)

27 April 1990: Seven teachers at Ely Community College will lose their jobs at the end of the summer term because the school can no longer afford to pay them – nominated for redundancy.

(*Times Educational Supplement*)

27 April 1990: the announcement that three senior teachers at an Essex secondary school are to lose their jobs has heightened fears that local management will lead to staff cuts throughout the county. More than forty of their colleagues have signed a petition saying that the cuts will over-burden the remaining staff.

(*Times Educational Supplement*)

18 May 1990: Rovert Guyver, the only primary teacher on the history National Curriculum working group, is about to lose his job at the school where he has taught for the past sixteen years. He has been nominated for redeployment. The school has to make savings of £5,000 to meet the county's new formula funding targets.

(*Times Educational Supplement*)

25 May 1990: Up to thirty teachers will be sacked in Oldham and Surrey due to what are thought to be some of the first compulsory redundancies caused by local management of schools. According to the NAS/UWT survey of 131 LEAs, a total of 756 teacher redundancies have been caused by the LMS. These include voluntary redundancies.

(*Times Educational Supplement*)

Another requirement of the Reform Act which is contributing to its culture-shock effect on teachers is open enrolment. This change is already making its impact felt in terms of the marketing of schools. Heads frequently experience greater pressures from this source than do their staff, so the effects on them are discussed in chapter 7.

But it is the National Curriculum initiative which is proving to be the biggest source of pressure from the Reform Act. Teachers' reactions have been varied and it is important to note the positive as well as the negative responses. Teachers have reported to me that they and their colleagues can benefit from the National Curriculum in these ways:

1 Teachers know what is expected of them from the clearly defined national curriculum, the standardized testing at 7, 11, 14 and 16, and the precise objectives carefully identified in the attainment targets and statements of attainment. These clearly defined expectations are a considerable relief to teachers who have just been through a major upheaval in their working lives and particularly if, before these changes, they felt that feedback on their performance as teachers was poor.

2 Increased job satisfaction and self-esteem can follow from an awareness of specific targets to guide teachers' work from positive feedback on their efforts. Their objectives are attainable and shared, so staff can say: 'we are all working for the same ends; we have a clear idea of what our colleagues are doing; parents and governors are increasingly interested in our teaching and share our goals; we have a growing sense of achievement.'

3 A third possible benefit comes from a clarification of teachers' roles in which professional boundaries are also defined more precisely. So teachers can say: 'we are not social workers or family guidance counsellors; our main commitment is to the national curriculum and we cannot become as involved as we were in the pre-Reform era in the numerous concerns arising from children's social and emotional development.'

This third benefit will be particularly appreciated by colleagues who share the views of one of the teachers on a course I conducted recently in Bristol University:

> I am expected to meet different and conflicting duties at once, e.g. those of a social worker, a baby-sitter, a parent and policewoman. I strongly feel those duties are not those of a teacher. I am fortunate to be a foreigner and to feel really remote to these problems. To keep my sanity and my priorities right I always remind myself that I was primarily trained to teach, impart knowledge, and that in no way am I qualified or trained to deal with my pupils' personal problems. I have a very different perception of my duties from that of my colleagues. I believe it is unethical to know too much about one's pupils. Of course I cannot ignore a disruptive or an unhappy child but I always make sure I am not too involved.

One of her colleagues on the course also expressed concern about the rapid expansion of roles based on the argument that all aspects of children's development – social, emotional, physical, moral, interpersonal and mental – should be accepted as the responsibilities of teachers (the 'whole child' approach). His conclusion was 'The role of the teacher has expanded to include social worker, psychiatrist, policeman and many other roles. Many teachers feel untrained and unable to deal with these pressures.'

There are good grounds for believing that these recent tendencies to widen teachers' areas of responsibility (another example is the identification of children who have been abused or who are at risk of child abuse) will now be slowed down, questioned and soon reversed as the impact of the current initiatives makes itself felt. Even though teachers who believe in the importance of the all-in model will struggle hard for its survival there will be strong factors working against them. One crucial factor is time. There is less available for the school concerts, trips, assemblies and Christmas parties which have been supported so enthusiastically by teachers and which have contributed to children's social development. Many extra-curricular activities have ceased and are lost to the pupils. There is less time to be concerned about the pastoral care of children and to gather information about their families.

The changes resulting from the implementation of the National Curriculum may also mean a major re-adjustment of how teachers in primary and secondary schools use their 1,265 hours. The National Curriculum requires them to devise schemes of work covering the core subjects, read and use what is described in *National Curriculum from Policy to Practice* (DES 1989) as 'a large amount of helpful material which NCC will be communicating to schools', participate in training and in the use of the new assessment procedures including selection and use of standard assessment tasks, make additional assessments, keep a record of pupils' progress in relation to each attainment target, hold moderation discussions with other teachers and provide information for parents.

To manage this very heavy load of changes requires more of teachers than the commitment asked for in the National Curriculum by DES. One teacher, who started with the process in her primary school in September 1988 told me:

> Organization and efficiency have never been so important. The Curriculum will involve the much better management of my time. Flexibility will still be there but there will be far more constraints.

The costs to her and her colleagues in preparing for these adaptations to their successful and satisfying working practices have already been considerable. They completed the annual required number of hours at the end of their first term and since then have been working at the same rate. But of equal or greater importance is the cost to a positive attitude to teaching. She said: 'I loved my job. But for the last three

Table 3.1 Obstacles to implementing the National Curriculum

Obstacle	Number of teachers	%
Lack of time	69	72·6
Large classes	16	16·.8
Poor resources	7	7·4
Lack of information	2	2·1
Poor pay	1	1·1
Poorly maintained buildings	0	0

months I have wanted to jack it in.' She fears that she will lose much of her all-in role because she believes that the implementation of the National Curriculum Attainment Targets will force teachers to balance the social, physical and emotional aspects of their pupils' development against their academic progress and she resents this very strongly. But she is willing, as a professional teacher, to support the National Curriculum even though 'It will take at least three years for me to see the true impact of the changes and the differences they have made both to me and the children I teach.'

Her work and that of her colleagues is becoming regulated by the four-item framework of the National Curriculum: profile components, attainment targets, levels of attainment and statements of attainment. They are learning to use a new terminology and new ways of curriculum planning, assessment and record-keeping as these apply to the core subjects of mathematics, science and primary English.

The time required for all these innovations cannot be extended because of the fixed number of hours specified in each teacher's contract. So, in school, time may be appropriated from non-essential activities as defined by the National Curriculum such as school visits and from non-core subjects such as careers and personal and social education. In this way core requirements may be subsidized by non-core hours. Outside school there will be a similar problem of appropriation but in this case the subsidizing will be from family time and the time previously given to sleeping, eating, exercise, relaxation, hobbies and holidays.

Some support for these ideas comes from a study of teacher time in Key Stage 1 conducted by two research workers and commissioned by AMMA. Each of the ninety-five teachers in the research project completed a time record for fourteen consecutive days from 7.00 a.m. to midnight (Campbell and Neill 1990). Their results indicated that in the teachers' experience the most serious obstacles to the implementation of the National Curriculum are identified in table 3:1. The research workers noted however that those teachers with classes of more than twenty-five pupils identified large classes as the most serious obstacle they were encountering in meeting the demands of the National Curriculum.

Their results also showed that fifty teachers were working more than 50 hours a week, while twenty were working more than 56 hours and ten were working more than 60 hours. But there was a great range of work time recorded, from more than 70 hours weekly to about half that amount. These differences in work time were largely accounted for in non-directed time in the evenings or at the weekend spent in marking or in preparation. The amount of time spent on these activities was not related to the positions of responsibility, age or experience. Campbell and Neill suggested an explanation that:

> a polarisation of attitudes to work may be developing between the 'conscientious' whose motivation is the traditional one in teaching where an attempt is made to meet all expectations to the best of one's ability. The alternative, perhaps newly emerged position, would be much more 'instrumental' – to limit time spent on work in the light of poor pay or of interests and responsibilities unconnected with work or of perceptions that to fulfil all expectations is an absurd demand.

This research has clearly highlighted the importance of motivators and demotivators for teachers. The major conclusion of the researchers was: the current reforms seem to depend very much on retaining the conscientiousness factor. If the conscientious teachers become smaller in number or become disillusioned the reforms are likely to fail' (Campbell and Neill 1990). They then identify a major demotivator which in their view 'is likely to increase stress and disaffection from the job'. This factor is a substantial imbalance in the distribution of a teacher's time between actually teaching in the classroom and non-teaching activities. They compare their results with a 1971 study (by Hilsum and Cane) which showed that 58 per cent of the time was spent on teaching and 42 per cent non-teaching. For the teachers in the 1990 study the proportions were almost completely reversed: 43.9 per cent teaching to 56.1 per cent non-teaching. Campbell and Neill believe that this change in the pattern of teachers' work with children is considered most significant for job satisfaction.

One of the primary teachers in my research made a similar point: 'There is a danger in primary schools of teachers having too many targets to aim at and too little time. Therefore the personal touches may go.'

Another possible demotivator has also been identified in a research study – the Primary School Teachers and Science research project based at Oxford (Redman *et al.* 1969). This investigation has revealed the conceptual difficulties which primary teachers can experience with scientific ideas and their feelings in relation to these difficulties – feelings of fear and inadequacy. The results of this investigation support the findings of other recent studies (Kruger *et al.* 1990) which have reported a mixture of enthusiasm and apprehension among primary teachers about the national curriculum and less confidence about their competence to teach science than in the case of other subjects.

A further significant demotivating factor engendering negative reactions to the National Curriculum is clearly presented by one of my Bristol University Students:

> Besides the very nature of teaching in Britain, legislative changes in education have greatly contributed to stress in the teaching profession. Many of the changes brought about have turned out to be very positive and yet the sheer powerlessness felt by British teachers has been such that many have rejected all changes altogether and asked for early retirement or left the profession or unfortunately broken down.

This teacher also noted that these changes may also represent an important alteration in status: 'Older teachers used to be able to have a great freedom of choice in their work. They now have to accept that they are employees who just do as they are told.'

This perception of a shift to an employee orientation from a professional role perspective may have important implications for the conscientious/instrumental differences in motivation identified in this chapter and so should be considered very carefully. In my view the change from a professional to an employee role started with the teachers' industrial action in the mid-1980s. At that time union loyalties were emphasized more strongly than before or since. During the period of industrial action staff were made aware of their contractual responsibilities by LEAs, one of which wrote to all its teachers: 'The Authority is paying its teachers to employ their professional skills in the fulfilment of its duty and responsibilities'. This emphasis on the employer–employee relationship was further emphasized in the same letter when the Authority warned, 'If a teacher's action takes the form of direct strike action for the whole or part of the school day . . . action by the Authority will include an appropriate reduction from salary by way of damages.'

A further shift in the direction of becoming an employee came with the abolition of the teachers' pay review body and its replacement by an 'advisory committee' and the loss of negotiating rights. The movement has grown stronger because of several elements in the Reform Act: changes in the membership, responsibilities and powers of governing bodies, leading to much greater control of schools including the cost of teaching and non-teaching staff; open enrolment with its increasing emphasis on market-place economics, for example the free-market competition between schools for pupils. This requirement of the Reform Act is already making schools aware that they have to compete with other schools for customers. As one head put it to his staff: 'We are going to have to sell ourselves to survive in a free market.' He might have added – 'We are salesmen and saleswomen.'

In my view this movement towards employee status is being encouraged also by the Local Management of Schools, with its itemization of teachers as a personnel cost in the school's budget. The National Curriculum is arguably making the strongest impact on teachers' perceptions of their roles, with its centrally controlled, standardized curriculum and testing which may considerably reduce the scope for staff to exercise their individual autonomy and encourage the feeling that they have no involvement in decisions which are made by central government and so their commitment (or conscientiousness) may be weakened. This feeling may be worsened by any further downgrading of their rights as professionals.

Some upgrading of teachers' rights and an increase in their commitment might have occurred if they believed that the Education Secretary had listened to their criticisms of assessment at Key Stage 1 and accepted their recommendations for reductions in assessment requirements. Their criticisms of the length, complexity and irrelevance of the pilot standard assessment tasks, the long hours of preparation and massive amount of paper-work and the practical problems of managing individual assessments while simultaneously dealing with a class all suggest a work overload quite sufficient to cause stress apart from all the other changes discussed in this chapter.

But there was no moratorium so that staff could assimilate the pre-Reform Act initiatives and prepare themselves for the Act. Nor did the long-standing inherent pressures of the job disappear. One of the most important of these is role conflict, and I tackle this concern in the next chapter.

4

PROBLEMS OF ROLE CONFLICT AND ROLE AMBIGUITY

In this chapter I shall support the argument that role conflict and role ambiguity are major sources of stress for staff. When teachers have pastoral care responsibilities as well as a teaching load these demands can lead to stress if they clash, for example a girl wants to talk to her tutor about a personal problem (a suspected pregnancy) when he is on his way to teach a sixth-form physics class. Role conflict is also experienced by teachers because they are aware of the expectations of parents, the media, LEAs and HMIs.

Two types of role conflict will be identified. The first arises because of contradictory expectations from other people, and the second from the contradictory roles that have to be reconciled in one appointment.

ROLE CONFLICT: CONTRADICTORY EXPECTATIONS

Role conflict occurs, for example, where the deputy head may be the 'piggy in the middle' between the headteacher, who may want to initiate changes, and staffroom colleagues, who may be resisting them. Role conflict of this type also occurs when parental expectations of pupil achievement, behaviour and attitudes are in conflict with staff expectations; often the head becomes the fulcrum for these opposing pressures, doing a precarious balancing act in the middle of the seesaw. Teachers may experience very different expectations of what their role should be, for example language teachers are confronted with markedly distinct interpretations of their job and the tension between these demands causes stress (Burke and Dunham 1982). Staff may have seasonal periods of increased pressures and conflict, for example music teachers heavily involved in the preparation and performance of Christmas music.

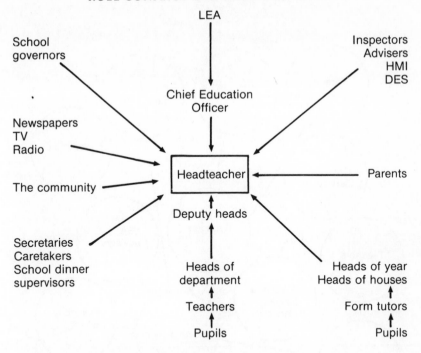

Figure 4.1 Sources of demands on headteachers in secondary schools

Headteachers and deputy heads

The demands on heads which can lead to this first type of role conflict can be illustrated by two analyses of their roles. The first, presented in figure 4.1, summarizes the expectations which secondary-school heads face from many different sources. The second, presented in figure 4.2, was completed by the head of a small primary school who had kept a record of all his face-to-face contacts during the previous school year.

The patterns of demands illustrated in figures 4.1 and 4.2 become more meaningful if they are set beside heads' reports of their role conflict. The following reports, of the heads of four different types of schools, are used as examples of this type of conflict. The head of a secondary school identified a wide range of pressures:

> The head is at the centre of all the internal and external transactions of the school, with the consequent need to make rapid adjustments when dealing with pupils, colleagues, governors, parents, meals staff and in my case a range of building contractors working on the site of this new school.

The head of an infants' school, on the other hand, experienced stress

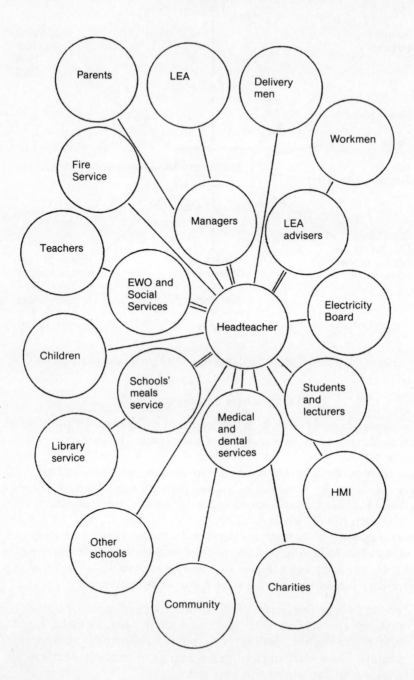

Figure 4.2 Sources of demands on a headteacher in a primary school

from heavy and disturbing pressures which were exerted on her from a parent and her LEA:

In my previous school when I was a fairly new head, I received a confidential letter from my County Education Officer stating that the LEA had received a letter of complaint from a parent over an incident which was supposed to have occcurred in the dining room – my 'force feeding' of a small child. I was asked to give my side of the story. My response to this was to phone the county office, as I could not recall this particular incident. The stress was aggravated when I was told to put my reply in writing and was also recommended to contact my professional organization. This left me feeling that the LEA believed the accusation made against me and did not intend to help me. Now with more experience I realize that such things happen to headteachers at some time in their life. I would recommend more publicity to potential headteachers to inform them that these things do happen to those in authority.

The headteacher of a middle school described his role as that of an intermediary between various interests, lobbies and disputants. He reported that the most frequent stress situations are those involving different sections of staff (teaching, cleaning, kitchen, secretarial) and parents. Those directly involving pupils seem to be more clear-cut. His greatest difficulty was concerned with situations in which a member of staff seemed justifiably criticized by pupils or parents. The conflict experienced by the headmistress of a small primary school was concerned with the demands of parents, teachers, pupils and administration. She was the first head of a new school on an estate, with Council and National Coal Board houses. To the head, the whole estate seemed 'anti-everything, especially anti-authority'. There were four working areas in the school (117 on roll) with a teaching head and three young teachers, one with two years' experience and the other two in their probationary year. The pressures of keeping these young members of staff from the irate attentions of various parents as well as coping with a class and the administration proved too much in the end for the head. She became ill, applied for another appointment and got it. The staff left with her.

Deputy heads are also subject to conflict because of contradictory expectations. This is experienced when they attempt to resolve the demands of day-to-day work and the need for long-term planning, that is, between the tactical and the strategic; between the minutiae and the helicopter-view. They are also exposed to expectations from different sources which often appear to be difficult to integrate. Deputies may be expected by the staff to 'belong' in the staffroom and to identify with and conform to staff norms. They may be expected by the head to identify with his or her aims and decisions rather than support the staff. These aspects of pressure on deputies can be seen in the following letter from the deputy head of a secondary school:

1 I'm responsible for buildings, furniture, etc. Often the repair is beyond my direct control and I am 'caught' between the legitimate demands of staff for quick action and the efficiency of contractors or the bureaucracy of the authority officers.

2 I'm responsible for nurturing community links. Staff criticize parents for wanting to discuss curriculum issues, parents criticize staff for not giving time to support events . . . etc. Gradually the show moves forward but its progress is slowed down by these kinds of issues.

3 Curriculum change is desired by some staff but not by others. Time is needed to woo the conservative group but the radicals are impatient. My job is to keep the waters calm, both sides talking and a goal in sight.

4 Eventually a discipline matter is referred to me. Staff who have already 'failed' are now critical of my success. They do not appreciate that now the context has widened and many people are involved.

These are just four examples but with one common theme. It is *people* who put pressure on me, people who impinge on me with different viewpoints, different demands and different expectations.

The role conflict of the deputy's job can also be identified in the report of a deputy head of a primary school who described the stress which she experienced after the appointment of a new head:

He was ten years younger than me and had no experience of working with infant or lower junior age children. At first the staff were welcoming but gradually tired of watching what they considered unwise decisions. Many of the staff were very experienced teachers and resentment grew. I was often asked to voice their dissent and this put me in a very difficult situation.

Heads of department

Heads of department may also experience this kind of role conflict when they act as intermediaries between their own department and other departments in the school or with the pastoral care heads of houses and years. Heads of department are thus required to act as negotiators pressing the claims of the members of their own departments, and defending their arguments. They may find that other heads of department and the pastoral heads are very sensitive when they think that anyone is encroaching on their particular areas of responsibility. Conflict may also be experienced with pastoral care staff, for example the head of a department might have to go through a pastoral care intermediary in order to contact parents when the intermediary might be a junior member of his or her department.

Heads of department are also the links between the teachers in their departments and the head. The staff may perceive this function to be to put their point of view to the head, while the head may perceive the head of department's role to have an important controlling function. These different perspectives and expectations with their potential for role conflict can be illustrated by the experience of a drama teacher in a comprehensive school. In her drama lesson she had been attempting to modify the unfavourable attitudes towards drama of 12- and 13-year-old boys and girls by discussing their own experiences and dramatizing them. The pupils, who had been very suspicious at the beginning of the school year, were now beginning to express their thoughts and feelings more fluently. Most of the group said they enjoyed these lessons. The teacher knew that the pupils wanted to continue this approach to drama. In her drama lessons in the hall the teacher was using unstructured situations which involved the building of a precariously balanced impromptu scaffolding of tables and chairs. The headmaster, passing by, saw this expression of 'creative drama' at its most exciting: the topmost part of the column was swaying, the children were considerably involved in the proceedings and the noise level was much higher than the norm for the school. At the end of the lesson the teacher was told by the head that what he had seen was not 'drama'. It was, he said, 'a group out of control'. The head of the English department was given the same comment. She was in the first year of her appointment and she was working hard to initiate changes in the teaching approaches used by members of the department. She thought that the head had agreed with her ideas when she was interviewed for the post. She had encouraged the young teacher to introduce the techniques but she now felt angry and disappointed by the head's remarks because she was now the 'woman-in-the-middle', being pulled and pushed in different directions by these contradictory role expectations.

Another source of role conflict for heads of departments can be found in the interaction between pupils, teachers and parents. A clear example of this kind of problem was provided by a head of department who gave me a detailed analysis of his role conflict:

To me Mr X seems incompetent; to the Adviser he is 'average'. He has failed on numerous occasions to supply marks, schemes of work, drafts of examinations, etc. He has constantly fallen behind on syllabuses, which makes life boring for the boys, without taking account of the deterioration in examination performance. He has been absent on flimsy excuses. He is late going to and leaving lessons. When he does take in work, it is returned eventually (three months is not rare) in a terrible state. The boys are painfully aware of the situation and the result is that they do not respect him and there is no successful working relationship – even the pupils think he is too easy-going. Complaints have been received from parents. Colleagues have noted that he helps in no way with any of the out-of-school activities. Transfer would seem to be the answer, but the Adviser does not think that this would be possible. The headmaster and I have discussed the matter fully and have tried all we can but quite simply we are victims of circumstances i.e. an inherited situation. I am worried because he teaches 40 per cent of the subject in the school and the subject will not get off the ground as long as he remains. Finally, where do we put him? Next year he will be teaching all the Year 7 and Year 8 classes and the bottom set of the Year 9, Year 10 and Year 11 forms, with only two periods with the sixth form seeing that he finds it impossible to maintain intellectual discipline and meet syllabus deadlines in the sixth form.

Incompetent teachers like Mr X increase the workload of heads of department to a significant degree. It is important, therefore, to note that there are now more opportunities than until quite recently to bring disciplinary proceedings against teachers whose professional performance is as bad as that of Mr X. Such proceedings can include dismissal (Barrell 1983). These actions may appear distasteful to some heads of departments and even disloyal to the members of their department. There is, therefore, the possibility of a clash of loyalties involving the individual teacher who may have been a colleague for some years, the other members of the department who may be bearing increased workloads, and finally the head because of strong parental pressures.

Pastoral heads

The conflicting demands which heads of department experience and which can make such a significant contribution to their stress also play a major part in the work pressures of the pastoral care heads (Blackburn 1983). Heads of houses and heads of year are presented with disciplinary and pastoral problems which require their attention and decisions. These problems may be presented urgently for immediate response in what appear to be crisis situations. They may be brought to their attention in the staffroom or when they are going to their lessons, since it appears to be common practice for pastoral care heads to carry a major teaching responsibility. These problems are clearly identified in the following report:

> As a head of house in a comprehensive school (14–18 years being the pupils' age range) I find one of the major stress situations occurs when important 'house business' has to be done when there is no real time to deal with it. Two days in the week especially seem to be more stressful than others. (a) Tuesday, our house duty day, when I am responsible for organizing staff and prefects' duties. I have two free periods but break times and lunch times are not really available for seeing pupils or colleagues. (b) Wednesday, when I teach every lesson and the day starts with our house assembly, which I have responsibility for organizing. Obviously things happen on these days which require urgent attention e.g. a pupil reported over a discipline matter, letters to write home, a reference or court report which needs to be written fairly urgently. One is faced with the choice of dealing with the problems immediately as soon as they come to light and thus neglecting one's other duties e.g. teaching, or delaying dealing with the problems until time is available. Each solution, or the compromise which often results, brings some anxiety or stress.
>
> Feverish activity often results; lack of concentration and patience in lessons is also possible. In general I feel that classroom teaching must come first, thus one is left with problems to deal with 'as soon as possible' (this can result in things being rushed due to lack of time, or in a significant delay occurring before any action is taken).
>
> There would seem to be no simple answer except unlimited free periods! The difficulty of course is that one can never know when the problems will come. If free periods were spread evenly through the week this would certainly help and if one had one 'free' each morning and afternoon the situation would be easier.

Other pastoral care heads are unable or unwilling to give the highest priority to their teaching commitments, with the consequence noted in a letter from a head of year in which he described his pressures and reactions. He also raised two other items of considerable importance in the development of occupational stress:

> I often arrive late for my lessons because of the demands of my year work. These include discipline and pastoral problems that need immediate attention, sick and injured children coming to the year room, parents on the telephone – the list is endless! And all the time I know that I have a class waiting for me and am hoping

that they are behaving themselves and, perhaps the most important of all, I have the worry of knowing that I am responsible for
their safety. A great deal of valuable school time is taken up with
Year 11 in providing references for employers etc. I sometimes
think employers are getting a very good service for nothing! Often
this service is provided at the expense of academic and year work.
Another problem is that year work, unlike academic work, is
sometimes difficult to measure in terms of success. This may in
turn cause frustration and stress.

The demands described in the above accounts, originating from different sources, are important causes of one kind of role conflict for
heads, deputies, and heads of department and pastoral care teams. But
another type can be found in these positions and should not be ignored.

ROLE CONFLICT: HAVING TO PLAY DIFFERENT ROLES

This conflict occurs because management posts contain several parts of
other people's roles which are very difficult to intregrate into a
coherent pattern. These include counsellor, careers adviser, social
worker, teacher, manager, resource provider, examiner, secretary,
restaurant manager, librarian and adviser. A head of year identified this
kind of role conflict with clarity and humour:

> The main pressure I experience is a result of my dual role as fairy
> godmother and wicked witch! On the one hand I have to deal
> firmly and forcefully with a 15-year old bully and yet appear as a
> sympathetic, approachable, caring person to his classmate in need
> of help or advice. Members of staff expect us to perform miracles
> – in the past we have had all classroom discipline problems passed
> on to us. This is changing gradually and heads of department are
> beginning to take these on, although we keep an overall view of
> students creating problems in several subject areas. The most
> difficult miracle to perform is rehabilitation of the social misfit –
> obviously a difficult task and in some cases impossible. Yet still
> colleagues refer these students to us with the instructions to 'sort
> out' so and so . . . he has BO/nobody likes him/he never utters a
> word to anyone/he sits on a wall on his own all lunchtime etc., etc.
> I inevitably attempt to engage this non-communicative individual
> in a two-way conversation and make what I vainly believe to be
> helpful suggestions to join the darts club/trampolining club, etc.

There is also another important area of pressure caused by conflict
between school and home demands. A head of department identified
this type of conflict as his major source of stress:

The main area of stress which affects me is the way at certain times of the year the job threatens to take over my whole life and with a variety of conflicting demands on my time, e.g. preparation and marking, administration, pastoral duties, meetings. I thrash around inefficiently, achieving little but yet spending ages doing it. I try and combat this by sitting down and planning my week, allocating time for each activity and building in some time for myself and my family each day. However, as pressures mount and fatigue sets in, the plans break down and more often than not it is my own time which is the casualty – hence resentment and added stress!

At such times also I feel the pressure of having to change roles so many times during the course of one day, of having to meet a variety of situations without sufficient preparation. This leads to what I believe is a familiar teacher's feeling of inefficiency and accompanying feelings of stress. Allied to this is also the lack of sense of achievement as one deals with so many things hastily and thus with limited satisfaction.

Finally, a problem I constantly grapple with and have yet to solve is that of sustaining a rich and varied life outside my work during term-time. I think this is important to provide balance and content-ment but especially as I get positions of more responsibility. I find the demands of the job, both in terms of time and energy, tend to work against other commitments. The resentment that this causes is perhaps the biggest source of stress I am finding at present.

I should be really grateful if you could include comment on one or more of these areas when you talk to us. I should like to write a little more fully but I am too busy at present!

Role expectations of heads of primary schools

A considerable number of role expectations can also be identified in primary schools, especially for heads. A major factor which has become more apparent recently is the increasing range of demands which are made on them for decisions about matters for which they have had little training or experience. This range includes electrical gadgets – calculators, tape recorders, projectors, computers, typewriters, pottery kilns and duplicating machines – carpentry jobs, boiler house mecha-nisms, cleaning equipment, playground fixtures and much else. The increasing complexity and sophistication of equipment in schools can be quite a problem – particularly when something breaks down or has to be replaced.

A head of a primary school recently listed, prior to one of my in-service courses, the jobs which she had been called upon to do during the last few months. It included the following: administrator, supply teacher, supply caretaker, secretary, first aider, building and safety inspector, technician, social worker, public relations expert, graphics expert, computer programmer, gardener and naturalist. She said that the list was not comprehensive and did not include such things as being the 'listening ear' when staff come to her with their personal, marital and emotional problems.

Another primary school head on the same in-service course reported a long list of role demands which she was expected to accept as legitimate parts of her position. She noted her problems under the heading:

Headteacher's problems and areas of stress

1 The headteacher often takes the role of social worker and problems range from potential suicide to looking after children (long after school hours) until the social services can provide overnight accommodation. As the only accessible 'professional' much of the head's time is spent listening to parents' problems connected with loneliness, marital breakdown or neighbour warfare.
2 Curriculum development and the attempt to change attitudes among staff and children can be difficult and putting new methods and ideas across to parents is a real problem.
3 Ordinary run-of-the-mill disaster days are those when the weather is poor, children are confined indoors, staff tempers are short, there is a queue of parents, a telephone rings incessantly and the headteacher has to take on the role of administrator, social worker, mother, nurse, secretary and teacher in turn. These days tend to get the adrenalin going but leave the headteacher exhausted.
4 Administration is a constant bugbear and tends to go to the bottom end of the priority list. Newsletters, forms in triplicate, school-fund accounts and letters to and from the LEA make heavy demands on the headteacher.
5 Perhaps the most frustrating area for me is the time spent on fund-raising activities, much of it in my own leisure time, and the need to sort out petty squabbles between parents who don't want to serve on the same stall at the fete or who complain because their children do not win prizes at the fancy dress parade. Having to be polite, friendly and full of gratitude to all-comers is absolutely exhausting.

For a third headteacher on this course there were different pressures, reminding us that while there are general role conflict situations for heads there are also important specific circumstances in different schools, communities and LEAs. For her, the main sources of role conflict were:

1 Multitude of daily trivia – phone calls, staff sick, unexpected visitors, naughty children, form-filling, etc., etc. – feeling like a second-rate juggler with too many balls in the air.
2 Dealing with a difficult member of staff or governor or a member of staff lacking competence – worrying whether I am putting in enough support.
3 Operating a watchful backdoor diplomacy to keep everything running smoothly despite chilly blasts from the media and the unease of staff.
4 The frustration of being in the position of enacting political will which you know is not conducive to good relationships within your school community.

ROLE AMBIGUITY

These areas of conflict for heads and members of senior and middle-management teams do not provide a complete description of the pressures arising from their roles. They have also reported role ambiguity as a major source of stress. This problem arises as a consequence of factors such as: lack of clarity about the scope and responsibilities of their job; uncertainty about what their colleagues expect of them; lack of information required to perform their tasks adequately; uncertainty about how their work is assessed and doubt about their own career opportunities.

Doubts and uncertainties about roles increase during periods of personal and organizational change. These may occur because of promotion and developments within a school following a new appointment. A head who had been promoted from a deputy's post wrote of his feelings of role uncertainty shortly after taking up his new post:

Without doubt the most stressful period was that between accepting the appointment and the first day of term. Although I visited the school on a number of occasions and talked at length with the existing headmaster and his deputies who were all most helpful, I had no sense of belonging to the organization. During the holiday period I visited the school regularly, but schools without pupils are strange animals and I felt a strong sense of isolation. Once the term began the only stress I noticed was that experienced before I addressed the first staff meeting on the first day. Again I had

41

the sensation of being a stranger entering a family gathering. After two weeks this feeling has largely disappeared and I am beginning to feel part of the organization rather than a decoration on top of the cake. The latter impression was caused because I was uncertain of my role. As a deputy, or in fact in any other post, I had known what was expected of me. As a new headmaster there was a distinct diminution of tasks to be accomplished.

For other heads, unfortunately, there is not the same reduction of ambiguity after promotion. Some of the possible effects of this problem can be identified in the report of a secondary-school head who had just completed the first 15 months of her headship:

A minority of staff have attempted to sabotage the system by outright antagonism to certain newly appointed staff and by becoming thoroughly unreasonable towards the pupils, both *en masse* and individually. The children are more reasonable, tolerant, loyal and forgiving than some staff. Some teachers are confused by consultation and long for a return to dictatorship and the 'close the doors and keep the nasty world out' syndrome. Stress comes from trying to maintain happy working relationships, not so much between the staff and me but between warring factions of staff. Stress also comes from a heavy teaching load, as we are 1.3 understaffed and the urge to teach well comes from the frustration of heading an expanding school in a contracting financial situation. The previous head didn't ask for things when money was available – now I'm asking I get sympathy and a reluctant 'no'. The workload is immense in a situation where a number of people are learning a new role and I'm chief trainer.

Historically, the head here has made all the decisions, and getting people to accept my delegated authority is exhausting. I am unable to stop working, at school and at home, therefore I have a very barren social life, which is destructive to me. I think this comes from the fear of not covering all eventualities. Even the most difficult members of staff have been moved to comment on my voracity for work and how tired I sometimes seem, but I cannot stop. It's a drive to prove that I am doing what they expected. I get depressed when I blame myself for a failure and at the end of a long bad day. I've never contemplated not going to school but I go sometimes with apprehension. Only very occasionally have I thought that if I had enough petrol in the car I would drive to Clifton and jump off the Suspension Bridge.

There are also frequent comments by teachers which suggest that the increasing pace of organizational and curricular changes in schools has resulted in major problems of role ambiguity and role conflict for staff. Some teachers are finding that the job they came into teaching to do is not the same job anymore – or, as many teachers have told me, 'the goal posts have been changed'. For some teachers, ideas about their role might have changed and they may feel their loyalties are not as strong as they were because the values which underpin their professional role have taken a significant shift towards the business ethic of the nineteenth century. The 'Baker Reforms' may seem, as they do to Philip Gammage, 'very like the Newcastle Commission Report (1861) – utilitarian, narrow and patronising'. (1988: 437). There are strong recommendations from Government, parents, school governors, media, industry and Local Education Authorities that the predominant values which should guide the performance of teachers' roles are those of market-place economics: cost effectiveness, cost cutting, profit and increased efficiency. The predominant theme is value for money. Free-market competition between schools for pupils in an open enrolment situation is becoming more overt as funding may depend on pupil numbers. These developments are anathema to teachers whose earlier professional experience was gained and enjoyed in a very different culture. These concerns are raised again in my final chapter, but meanwhile in the next chapter I want to investigate a further source of stress – the pressure of children's behaviour and attitude.[3]

5

PRESSURES OF CHILDREN'S BEHAVIOUR

This chapter is concerned with a number of pressures concerned with children's behaviour which teachers describe as disruptive, troublesome, aggressive, maladjusted or disaffected (Jones 1989) and which they believe is often caused by emotional or behaviour disorders (Mongon and Hart 1989). These labels are given to a wide range of behaviours from the pupil who refuses to co-operate and does little or no work in class to the child who is openly aggressive towards other children and teachers. This range can be seen in a survey conducted among teachers in Clwyd in which disruptive behaviour was analysed into six categories which were listed in order of occurrence as : rowdyism, actual violence, damage to property, threats of violence, theft and sexual misbehaviour. Rowdyism was defined as 'deliberate lateness to lessons, disturbance in the lessons, verbal abuse and refusal to co-operate' (Clwyd County Council 1976).

A survey of what teachers described as disruptive behaviour was also conducted in two London secondary schools by Lawrence, Steed and Young (1983). When these teachers talked about acts of disruption they meant rowdyness, abuse, bad language, talking and refusing to accept the teacher's authority. In these schools disruptive behaviour did not take the form of violence and aggression against teachers. This extreme type of disruption is reported in other investigations, however, and these reports suggest that violent and aggressive behaviour makes demands on teachers which range from minor infractions to incidents that stretch their coping methods to their limits – and sometimes beyond them.

Specific examples of children's behaviour which make different demands on staff have been given recently by McManus (1989). His list includes:

Arriving late

Tapping other pupils
Asking to go to the toilet repeatedly
Missing lesson, absconding
Smoking in toilets
Rude remarks under breath
Pushing past teacher
Refusing to do set work
Playing with matches in class
Running on corridor or stairs
Cheeky/joky remarks to teacher
Talking when meant to be writing
Keeping coat on in class
Chasing round room
Fighting others in class
Open abuse to teacher
Setting off fire alarm
Throwing pencil across room
Talking when teacher talking
Packing up early, as if to leave
Unauthorized drawing on book
Taking pupil's property
Failing to bring homework
Unruly on way to school
Taking teacher's property
Grafitti on corridor wall
Damaging classroom fittings
Bizarre clothing/make-up
Rocking on chair defiantly
Hitting teacher
Fighting in yard
Threatening teacher
Swearing at pupil in class
Attempting smoking in class
Refusing punishment
Leaving class early.

But the most extensive and influential investigation of the causes and effects of disruptive behaviour in the 1980s was the Elton Report (DES and Welsh Office 1989) of the results of an enquiry into discipline in schools in England and Wales and the recommendations of Lord Elton's committee in the light of their findings. Part of the enquiry consisted of a research study by the Educational Research Centre at the University of Sheffield of 'teachers' perceptions and concerns about discipline'. The results of this research indicated that the most disturbing pupil behaviour experienced by teachers included talking out of turn, hindering other pupils, making unnecessary noises, work avoidance, not being punctual and getting out of seat without permission.

When these examples of disruptive behaviour are compared with more serious problems such as verbal abuse or physical aggression towards teachers, physical aggression towards pupils or vandalism they appear minor and perhaps even insignificant as causes of stress. This might be true if they were isolated incidents. But for some teachers they cause frequent frustrations and hassles during the working day. A recent survey carried out by researchers from Birmingham University's Centre for Child Study concluded that 'teachers are in general much more concerned about persistent minor misbehaviour than the occasional dramatic confrontation' (Houghton, Wheldall and Merrett 1988). The Elton Committee described these difficulties as 'persistent low level classroom disruption' and noted that the survey of teachers' experiences carried out for their enquiry by Sheffield University's Educational Research Centre indicated that 'the vast majority of primary and secondary teachers reported that the flow of their lessons (in the previous week) had been impeded or disrupted by having to deal with minor discipline problems and one in four teachers had also to deal with misbehaviour outside the classroom every day'. Verbal abuse towards other pupils and 'cheeky or impertinent remarks or responses' were encountered frequently in the previous week by the primary and secondary teachers in the survey. Primary colleagues report 'physical aggression towards other pupils as a special concern'. The interviews which the research workers had with these teachers about incidents of misbehaviour led them to conclude that 'their cumulative effects are wearing and contribute to a sense of stress and growing frustration'.

A survey conducted in his comprehensive school in 1989 by a head of department on my Bristol University course for middle managers in secondary schools suggests that 'persistent minor misbehaviour' is the major source of stress for some colleagues. The results of his small-scale school-based investigations were presented in the following table:

Rank-order of major sources of occupation stress for teachers in an
Avon comprehensive school

1 Pupil misbehaviour
2 GCSE coursework marking
3 Lowering of professional standards because of workload
4 Lack of adequate resources for the job
5 Too many irrelevant meetings
6 Large class sizes

7 $\left\{\begin{array}{l} \text{Feeling undervalued} \\ \text{Low morale amongst staff} \\ \text{Pupils arriving late for lessons} \end{array}\right.$

A much larger survey of occupational stress among teachers which used a United Kingdom sample of colleagues was reported a year later by two UMIST research workers (Travers and Cooper 1990). They identified the ten top sources of pressure on staff:

1 Lack of support from government
2 Constant changes
3 Lack of information about these changes
4 Lack of respect for teachers
5 National Curriculum
6 Salaries out of proportion with workload
7 Pupil assessment
8 Pupils' behavioural problems
9 Lack of non-contact time
10 Lack of relation between teaching skill and promotion.

These surveys indicate that pupil misbehaviour is still one of the major sources of stress for teachers and recommendations for the management of misbehaviour are discussed in my last chapter. It would be misleading, however, to conclude that teachers are experiencing only the minor forms of misbehaviour. It is evident from the Elton Committee Report and from other sources that more serious incidents occur. The Sheffield Educational Research Centre's investigation for the Elton Committee found that in the week of their survey 'More than one in ten secondary teachers and more than one in twenty primary teachers had had verbal abuse directed toward them by pupils.'

Some of the effects of these difficulties were reported by a teacher in one of my recent Bristol University workshops. He sent the following note to his colleagues:

As part of my course we are looking at stress in teaching. If you have had a stressful experience or find a particular part of your work stressful I would like to hear about it. (In strictest confidence of course – no names necessary.)

One of the responses to this request for information gives us a clear insight into the strong reactions of some teachers to severe misbehaviour in their classrooms:

Being constantly expected to exercise exceptional self-control. For one's own sanity and health, you learn the skill of humouring a foul-tempered child or diffusing a potentially difficult or violent situation. Remaining calm when the normal reaction would be to scream back or be equally abusive. Being driven to extremes of anger that are alien emotions by children who are being deliberately provoking. You are fully aware of what they are trying to do and you fight to remain controlled.

Physical aggression towards teachers was also discussed by the Elton Committee and they noted that 'Around one in fifty primary and secondary teachers also reported having to deal with some form of physical aggression directed towards them during the course of the week' (of the survey).

An insight into the effects on staff of having to cope with aggressive behaviour may be obtained from some of the incidents which have been reported to me. They indicate severe problems in all types of schools. The following two reports are concerned with the behaviour of infant school children. The details were given to me by their teachers for a staff conference which I organized for an in-service training day. The first problem was described by the teacher as an extremely disruptive boy who joined the class in mid-term and caused total disruption. He tore pictures from the wall, threw children's games across the room, scribbled over their work and painting and could not sit beside children without doing something to them. He pinched their faces, pulled their hair, kicked or punched them and put his hand up girls' skirts. If he felt the least bit rejected or ignored he would inflict injury on himself. Usually this would be biting and scratching his hand until he drew blood. He would scream with pain but refuse to take his hand out of his mouth. The children in the class were petrified of him to begin with and used to keep as far away from him as possible. The teacher said she had to keep an eye on him for every second of the day and was under extreme stress for the whole of the time he was in her class.

In the same school one of her colleagues was attempting to cope with another aggressive boy. She gave me some details of his behaviour:

His aggressive sessions were usually triggered off by a small and apparantly trivial incident. He began by hitting one of the other children and when I intervened his behaviour became increasingly violent. He kicked everything in range. He threw furniture around the room and knocked over anything which stood in his way. He screamed abuse at the top of his voice. My first concern when a mood took him was to get myself between him and the other children. Sometimes I dragged him into the classroom and let him give vent to his pent-up feelings by kicking and punching the walls, the floor and the doors. Sometimes I tried to hold him, having first removed his shoes, which was no easy task. When I reached the end of my tether I sent one of the children for the headmistress who tried to take him back to her room. The main areas of stress were the uncertainty of not knowing when he would react like that, the bites, cuts and bruises.

The next report of a severe incident is concerned with a child in a primary school which was sent to me by the headteacher. The boy, 'Johnny', was 11 years old and had been in the school two and a half years. He was known by the staff as a 'loner' and as a boy who was not popular with his peers. The incident which the head described had happened a week before my in-service training day for the primary school heads in an LEA. One of the dinner supervisors had told Johnny and another boy to stop fighting. Johnny then ran off. The dinner supervisor asked for the assistance of a teacher because she thought that Johnny had run away from school. The teacher found the boy by one of the school gates in a very sullen mood and he seemed quite unprepared to chat with the teacher or co-operate in any way. The teacher asked Johnny to go inside the building but Johnny lost his temper and threw a tantrum. He clung to the railings in an act of defiance. When the teacher managed eventually to get the child into the building and sit him down, he was still in the most uncooperative frame of mind. The dinner supervisor had told the teacher that Johnny had been abusive to her when she had asked him to stop bullying a younger child. But, according to Johnny, the dinner supervisor had not understood that they were fighting in a friendly way rather than in a temper.

During the interview with the teacher Johnny was gasping and catching his breath the whole time. He was taken to his classroom and asked to sit down at his desk. He did so and appeared to be calmer. A little while later the teacher checked that he was still in his classroom and found at the time that Johnny was crunching something in his mouth. As he told the teacher that he had eaten his dinner, he was then asked what he was eating. He showed the remains of a pencil and the teacher, to quote his own words, 'was staggered to see his mouth was crammed full of pencil and that he was apparently eating it'.

In the secondary school some of the severest forms of behaviour which teachers have to contend with can be illustrated by the report to me by the head of house in a comprehensive school of two boys aged 14 and 15. The 14-year old's behaviour was described by the head of house as extremely disruptive, and he gave details of what he meant by this description:

> He came to us at the beginning of the second year. He was placed in a remedial form but even here he is well behind other children. Progress is very slow and he retains little but he has occasional flashes of insight. He is extremely disruptive and often downright dangerous in practical lessons. He *will* not sit still and in fact jogs

and dances round the room. Even when he is seated he continually mutters and talks to himself and others and he is often obscene and aggressive to staff. He is a bully (a big boy for his age) sometimes just for the sake of it, e.g. making other boys eat cigarettes – or worse; but more often in order to extort money (or anything else he takes a fancy to) from other children. However it is very difficult to prove this as most children are too frightened to complain. For the sake of the other children and after much deliberation we requested that he be removed from the school. However the parents absolutely refused even though they had no control over the boy. Being part of the school is obviously benefitting the boy himself. He loves school, was very proud to take part in sports day and to play rugby for the school. Unfortunately it is the other children who are suffering while he gains, socially, academically and financially.

The 15-year-old boy had created many problems at school such as petty theft and the more serious stealing of dangerous chemicals from the school laboratories. He disrupted lessons by refusing to work. He wrote obscene letters to the staff and gave details which meant they could be easily traced to him. He suspended smaller pupils from second-storey windows by their hands. He broke into school at the week-end and vandalized the main offices. During his illegal time in school he let off the fire extinguishers. In his report to me, the head of house tried to analyse why the behaviour of these two boys caused him so much stress:

In my position as head of house I have to try and balance the pupil's interest against the staff and the philosophy of the school. This has led to confrontation with junior staff, senior staff and finally the head. In many instances the staff found the pupil's antics to be highly amusing, e.g. pretending to be a dead fly during art lessons. However when indiscipline crept in the staff gave up and wanted me to deal with it. Parental support for the boy was negligible. The final conflict was a head-on clash with the head over the pupil's suspension, which resulted in disciplinary action against myself being threatened. The pupil was suspended on many occasions and put into a unit for disruptive pupils. I felt that I was always fighting a losing battle against the staff, who were not interested in the long-term problems.

The role conflict of heads of house and year who experience the opposing forces of staff, headteacher and pupils and parents presents major problems because the feelings aroused by children presenting severe behaviour problems can be very strong. These children are often very angry and so their teachers often encounter what one of them described as 'raw emotion', from a number of children in and out of class. This strong emotion may be expressed in different ways: aggressiveness, attention-seeking behaviour, a lack of consideration for other people or unfriendly attitudes towards them. For teachers who do not think that teaching is concerned with the raw emotions of anger the expression of it in classroom or school can be a distressing experience. For teachers whose personal values and experience have led them to believe that the right way to deal with angry feelings is to 'swallow' or hide them it can be a frightening experience to be faced with children and young adults who do not seem to share their inhibitions. These teachers are sometimes out of their depth emotionally and therefore another major source of stress in teaching children with emotional or behavioural disorders is insecurity, which is increased by the unpredictability of the pupil's behaviour. This perspective was clearly formulated by a perceptive teacher who wrote:

Insecurity is the cause of much stress amongst the people I work with and it appears to be the result of the unpredictability of the behaviour of the children. The staff rarely know exactly what to expect next and this threatens their security by reducing their control over their environment. This insecurity is increased by direct confrontations with children, especially when they are hostile as a group towards us, either individually or collectively and they do naturally exploit this. Another source of insecurity is lack of psychological knowledge, a feeling that one is out of one's depth with a particular child. This is particularly pertinent when an adult is faced with a hostile reaction which is not understood; the adult then tends either to feel intellectually inadequate, or worse still, can take a hostile reaction personally.

A further source of insecurity for teachers is that the range of the pupils' behaviour and attitudes is beyond the teachers' experience, training and expectations. In these circumstances staff working with me say that they feel confused and uncertain about the right actions to take. These pressures can be identified in the following comment, which ends with a question asked frequently:

He is a Year 7 boy who is an overweight and unattractive child. He continually pesters staff at every opportunity and demands attention with repetitive questions. He is inclined to daydream in class but pretends to work hard. Older children plague him and every playtime he seeks refuge by following the staff on duty. He seldom plays with his peers but when he does he causes embarrassment by touching and kissing them and by making

51

occasional declarations of love. His is the youngest child of overbearing parents. What can we do to help him now before our patience has worn thin?

I was invited into this boy's school to discuss with the tutors of the Year 11 pupils some of the problems caused by their behaviour and attitudes. They presented me with the following list which the tutors said contained the names of the children they did not understand and wanted help with:

Brian He is the youngest of four children. He has a record of truancy, lying, theft, idleness and disruptive behaviour. He is definitely under-performing though it is thought by the staff that he is certainly not as clever as his father believes. Father is repressive and unsympathetic with the son and argues with the mother in front of the boy: he blames the school for not making the boy work harder. If Brian does any homework his father demands to see it and on one occasion tore it up after telling his son that it was rubbish. The boy now only works when forced to by the staff. The subject teachers find it difficult to give him the attention he needs. They are often thankful if he is quiet. What do you suggest?

Joyce She first became awkward towards the end of Year 7, when she started avoiding PE. Throughout the second year she refused to take part in this subject. During the third year she was frequently in trouble for lateness and smoking and often ran home after a confrontation. On one of these occasions she bit the senior mistress. She now became a serious problem, seldom managing to complete a full day in school and she was shoplifting during these absences. Throughout her school 'career' the parents were consulted regularly but with no real co-operation. Mother refused to accept that there was a problem even though she had no control over the child herself. She had also been seeing the Educational Psychologist who eventually decided she should be 'statemented' and should not be in our school. However in practice this made little difference as there were no places available in schools for her. Joyce says that she hates this school. The head of another school was persuaded to accept her on the condition that she put in a full week's attendance with us. So far she has not put in a full day!! Where did we go wrong?

Neil He belongs to an upper-middle-class family. He is under-achieving and will gain fewer exam successes than he should. He is often abstracted in class. On the cover of one of his exercise books he wrote recently:

'I don't know and I don't fucking care. I'm going to kill me mum

and dad and tear out all my hair. KILL   KILL   KILL'
Do we take this seriously?

A head of house in the same school argued on one of my courses that for staff in positions of responsibility, particularly in pastoral work, stress was inevitable because teachers had to become involved in the pupils' problems. To avoid stress it was necessary to remain uninvolved and 'to walk past the non-uniformed pupil, the disruption, the fights, the litter and all those day-to-day events which create stress'. But if the teacher did this he argued, he or she would be useless in the job.

When involvement in the pupils' behaviour is matched by concern for the pupils' problems, teachers experience further stress because they feel they can do little to help the pupils to cope with the pressures which make them disruptive. Members of staff report that they feel helpless and hopeless because they are powerless to change the conditions in which the children live. Some the these circumstances were identified in a research project carried out by a deputy head in Northampton (Bispham 1980). He interviewed pupils in secondary schools who had been reported by their headteachers to have behaviour problems; a few brief statements from his interviews provide an outline of the daily heavy pressures they experience:

> I look out of our front door at the street and wonder if I'll ever manage to get away from it all. There must be a different sort of life somewhere. My home is all untidy and nobody knows what's going on. That's why I like school to be orderly and well organized. Homework is alright for a lot of kids, especially when you've got small families and the parents understand. But tell me, how do you think I get it done in a place like ours? The kids tear the books and get jam on everything. Telly never stops. 'Use your bedroom' says the teacher. Is he kidding, it's even worse there and I share it with two others. Homework isn't very realistic for a lot of us. Is it really necessary?

The feelings of impotence which teachers may develop as they learn about these circumstance were clearly formulated by a head teacher in a primary school in response to my request for information about the stress situations she experienced in school:

> Some days I despair of the future when I see the pupils' home circumstances. Some of the children just haven't got a chance. That's when I get a feeling of deep frustration and wonder if anything I have tried to do will have any long-term effect.

A teacher in a secondary school built in a big council estate had resigned because she could no longer cope with the work pressures she identified for me before my staff conference in her school. She wrote:

> The causes of stress for me are the poor discipline in pupils, particularly the coarse language; unsolicited rudeness and constant talking; losing free periods which are needed for preparation, duplicating etc; having to cover for a colleague who is not pulling her weight; noise and the constant battle to create a stimulating but tranquil and ordered environment in the classroom. I feel I'm a zoo-keeper, not a teacher. My initial reaction is to laugh it off and turn the whole thing into a joke. This leads to some very cruel 'fun' in the staffroom – I hear myself expressing attitudes which basically are against my principles. Deep down one feels a sense of outrage and anger that schools like this should exist. Underlying all this is a terrible sense of sadness at having to witness wasted lives and opportunities.

The feelings of not being able to make an adequate contribution to the solution of the pupils' problems are compounded by communication difficulties between teachers and other professional workers. The children who are disruptive in school have often also come to the attention of the police, probation officers, child guidance clinics, health and social services and therefore the disruptive pupil is often a multi-disciplinary problem rather than an educational one. But inter-professional contact and communication can be ineffective and frustrating rather than supportive (Dunham 1981b, Cleveland Inquiry Report (Butler-Sloss 1988)). One teacher in a secondary school put the matter bluntly:

> There are too many people who offer hypothetical advice. When we seek support beyond the bounds of the school, too often the problem is referred back to us as though we had done nothing to deal with the problem.

There are also reports of communication difficulties leading to feelings of a lack of support within a school. A team of research workers (Galloway *et al.*1982) who investigated the effects of special classes for disruptive pupils in Sheffield wrote:

> Teaching can be an extraordinarily lonely profession. The loneliness of the classroom is compounded by that of the staffroom. Disruptive behaviour is the most striking example of stress which too often has to be borne in painful isolation. For many teachers, admitting to bad classroom discipline is paramount to admitting that they are bad teachers.

So there may be an absence of support for staff teaching disruptive pupils, as their colleagues may feel reluctant to offer assistance because to do so would imply their colleagues' incompetence. Many who join my in-service courses appear not to have experienced much support in their schools. They seem to have had few opportunities to discuss their stress situations. They seem surprised to find acceptance and not cynicism as they are encouraged to express their feelings and release their emotional blocks. A head of department in a comprehensive school told me of her expectations before she came to one of my courses and her growing awareness of an alternative approach to teachers who want to talk about their problems:

> As a result of previous experience I came with a guarded attitude and I feel I was aggressive towards you at times, something for which I apologise. In fact I thought you were most caring in the way you posed your penetrating questions and comments. I was glad to be made aware without being made to feel inadequate, criticized or condemned as had been my previous experience in school. I certainly feel more able to cope and more willing to lend a sympathetic ear to those who feel at the end of their tether.

The difficulties which staff experience with their colleagues in relation to the teaching of disruptive children have another dimension. It may be thought by some staff that to a significant extent school policy and teaching behaviour are responsible for the disruptive pupils' behaviour. The research of the deputy head in Northampton (Bispham 1980) which was discussed earlier in this chapter provides some information in support of this argument. A few brief statements from his interviews will indicate what I mean:

> There's eight of us stick together all the time. We cause a lot of trouble but they still leave us together. Maybe they don't care anyway.

> This school pretends. It doesn't really care about anybody. It's just a face it puts on.

> I suppose I was disappointed with the third, fourth and fifth years. It was all the same thing with the same equipment but not enough of it. In fact it was the same old making do.

> Men accept me as a woman. I know men fancy me and I enjoy it. But here I'm just another silly little kid.

> Sometimes a teacher calls me 'shorty' or 'fatso'. It isn't fair. I hate it and I try to pay them back.

Support for the point of view that a school's organization and relationships are important factors in the development of disruptive behaviour can also be found in the report of the study of special classes for disruptive children in ten Sheffield secondary schools referred to earlier (Galloway *et al.*1982). The research team found large differences between these schools in the number of incidents reported by staff which caused them 'genuine concern or stress extending beyond their day-to-day problems'. At one school 33 per cent of the teachers interviewed could not think of an incident which had caused them real concern in the current school year (most of the interviews took place in the spring term). In contrast over 85 per cent of teachers at two other schools could think of disruptive incidents which had caused them real concern in the present term. Frequently the incident was within the previous two weeks. The teachers in the ten schools were asked about sources of support in dealing with disruptive behaviour. In six schools the formal channels for dealing with problem pupils involved referral upwards – teachers were expected to refer to the head of department or to the year tutor, who if necessary would 'hand on' the pupil to the deputy head, who in turn would pass the problem on to the head teacher. Staff tension and frustration developed because these channels were found to be unsatisfactory: they were too slow; they did not give enough support to teachers at the rough end of the pupil's behaviour; and it was felt that senior staff did not appreciate their difficulties. In these schools it was implied that asking for help was a sign of weakness.

In the schools with the smallest number of reported incidents it was a firm aspect of school policy that the form tutor was much more than the first point of referral: this was the point of the first action. It was therefore necessary for the tutor to know not only the pupils in the tutor group but also their parents. It was also strongly emphasized that effective school policy for coping with problem behaviour depended on consultation between staff. The Sheffield team gives an illustration of these two approaches in their report of a form tutor whose problem was that a girl with an Italian mother was being called a 'Wop bitch' and other offensive names. The tutor told the senior mistress about her concern. She was advised to deal with the matter in her tutor group. She talked to the girls involved and the problem was resolved without escalating it upwards to a higher management level. The tutor received support and encouragement in dealing with the problem herself and so her confidence was strengthened.

The importance of support for staff has been emphasized more recently in the report of violence towards teachers by the Health and Safety Commission in November 1990. These violent incidents included 'severe kicks to the head when separating two fighting 9 year olds and punches to the arms when disciplining a 15 year old girl'. The Commission recommended that teachers who are the victims of verbal abuse and physical violence might need time off work, counselling or compensation. But their most important recommendation was that support systems should swing into action automatically! This appeal for staff support to help colleagues manage disruptive behaviour indicates how important it is to consider whole school approaches in terms of the guidelines proposed by the Elton Committee. These will be discussed in the last chapter but meanwhile in the next chapter I want to consider the exacerbating effects on staff of poor working conditions.

6

PROBLEMS CAUSED BY DIFFICULT WORKING CONDITIONS

When the environment in which teachers work is poor three important kinds of pressures are generated: physical, financial and organizational. The physical aspects of poor working conditions include badly constructed buildings with inadequate sound-proofing and high noise levels, and split-site schools with the consequent difficulties of commuting between buildings. The financial aspects are becoming increasingly significant. Reduced school budgets have meant lower levels of expenditure on equipment and textbooks and smaller LEA funds have resulted in the redeployment of teachers, redundancies, school closures, narrowing of promotion opportunities and the restriction of career prospects. The organizational aspects include difficult and frustrating staff relationships which may result in little support of junior staff by top management, poor co-operation between the academic and pastoral concerns and conflict between departments and teams and between cliques in the staffroom. The major consequences of poor communications include conflict about different aspects of school policy and time pressures because of poor planning of issues such as meetings and deadlines. These organizational pressures are often related to the management styles of the head and deputies.

The continuing importance of difficult working conditions can be noted in the following survey of the pressures on staff of a comprehensive school which I compiled for a staff development conference from information I was given by the teachers:

Disruptive and unmotivated pupils
Senior management
Meetings
Paperwork
Working conditions
Capitation allocation
Lack of consultation

Directed time arrangements
Assembly and registration
New initiatives introduced too quickly
Time pressures

The many-sided aspects of difficult working conditions are delineated in this vivid review by a teacher in a comprehensive school:

> The biggest source of pressure in this school, built in 1888, is the physical lack of space, within and without the building. The classrooms have high windows, the playground space is limited and there is no grassy area. The hall which is in use all day and contains the PE climbing equipment, also serves as a dining area and there is a shortage of tables and chairs. We have new exciting equipment which requires storage in an easily accessible place. Finding a place proves extremely difficult and entails constant re-thinking. The display of children's work uses space which is at a premium and which needs to be carefully thought out to avoid damage. The lack of space is, of course, accentuated by high class numbers. The dinner hour causes pressure, as most of the children stay either for lunch or sandwiches and there is pressure throughout the morning and afternoon breaks with so many children to supervise. The large numbers prove also very difficult for untrained welfare ladies to manage, which gives rise to tension.

New schools also confront teachers with inadequate working conditions. The need to save money on building costs has resulted in the erection of poorly constructed buildings with inadequate sound insulation between classrooms. Some teachers express anger at being disturbed, some are resentful of their colleagues' criticisms about the talking and movement they allow in their classes, while others react to high levels of noise apathetically. Newly built primary schools have tended to incorporate open-plan designs. Here too, higher noise levels have been reported and their possible significance in the development of stress has been identified by the headteacher of a first school who reported that her two most stressful years in teaching were those spent as deputy head of a new open-plan infant school. Stress was caused by a number of factors: she did not agree with the head's organization of the school but because of her sense of loyalty she did not criticize her; she was experimenting with a new method of teaching reading which gave disappointing results; the open-plan design forced her to change her accustomed teaching patterns as she had to work closely with another member of staff, which brought complications but little benefit. Her summary of these two years was: 'I became accustomed to the complications but I always found the noise excessively tiring'.

Table 6.1 Decibel levels of some sources of noise

Noise Source	*Noise Levels in Decibels*
Plane taking off	120
Road menders using drills	100
A really busy road	80
Someone talking to you at a normal level	40–50

Source: Guardian 4 December, 1990, p. 10)

There are research reports of further consequences for people who work in prolonged noisy environments, though little attention has been given to their possible harmful effects in schools. Research in industry has established that noise can damage hearing and can have psychological effects of poor concentration and sudden changes of mood. The damage to hearing is related to the gradual development of chronic deafness and a person is at risk of this disability after exposure to noise levels exceeding 90 decibels. The noise levels in decibels of different noise sources are given in Table 6.1.

It is helpful to compare these decibel counts with the results of monitoring school noises. In one inner-city secondary school where I participated as the consultant in a staff development conference, daily records were kept for a week by the local Environmental Health Officer and showed decibel counts of 65 – 75. In a new comprehensive school the noise level of one particular source was monitored and reported to me by a head of department:

> We have a system of bells which serve to signal the end of lessons and as fire alarms. Recently an over-zealous Fire Officer decreed that bells, which have been adequate for the dual purpose for twenty years, must be replaced with gongs designed for external fire alarms. These have been installed on landings, where children are constantly interviewed by staff and in our newest building over the teacher's blackboard. One of these measures 102 decibels at six feet. It is a source of actual pain and dread.

These reports suggest the importance of considering noise as a contributory factor in the development of stress. But there is one more stress situation which should be identified before this discussion of the physical aspects of poor working conditions is concluded. This is concerned with the erection of widely spaced buildings in new schools and the use of existing buildings on different sites as split-site schools.

Teachers here have to contend with what is described as a 'brisk five minute walk between lessons carrying books and equipment' or a 'sharp ten minute drive in the car to the main building'. An example of the difficulties which can be caused by split-site working was presented by the deputy head of a secondary school:

> The staff managed fairly well if they could be away from the main school all morning or all afternoon but this was not always possible and much time was spent travelling to and fro, carrying books, etc., which was tiring especially if it was wet. Pastoral care/communications between staff or staff and girls were not always adequate, staff absence and cover were much more difficult to arrange, especially when it concerned staff without cars, as the day-to-day contact with each other was severely diminished.

The negative effect on colleagues of working in some of today's schools because of unsatisfactory physical conditions can be seen in the following brief comments from staff in a comprehensive school:

- Too much unnecessary movement
- Too much noise
- Inadequate teaching environment
- Depressing decorative state of the interior of the school, i.e. unpainted walls, torn floor coverings, marked desks and table tops and window blinds damaged
- Doors that won't close and drawers that won't slide.

The second kind of evironmental pressure which teachers are having to cope with is financial. The effects can be recognized in the deterioration of some of the physical aspects of the school but most directly they have been felt in the classroom. The lack of money for school resources has hampered the development of new courses and has blocked the use of updated textbooks. But the contraction of the Education Service has placed more general burdens on staff. The staff of a secondary school identified several of these aspects of their difficult working conditions:

- There will only be one Computer Studies group next year even though that means refusing some students who have already applied for the course.
- My pay is lousy.
- There is little opportunity to move to other schools.
- Lack of adequate resources and teaching facilities.

Many staff are affected by radical changes in career expectations, particularly those teachers who entered the profession with a vertical model of achievement based on promotion. In the early part of their careers this model matched reality: they were for example promoted to middle-management positions in their late twenties or early thirties with the strong assumption that further progress would follow. These assumptions are no longer valid and a painful analysis of their professional and personal development is a common theme in my discussions with them. These risks of non-promotion to middle management and senior management positions are presenting entirely new kinds of problems to colleagues whose whole previous work experience has been spent in a period of expansion.

The third kind of environmental pressure is organizational. Here, the problems include ineffective communications, difficult staff relationships, very heavy workloads and inappropriate leadership styles. Explicit details of these difficulties were reported and discussed by colleagues in an in-service conference. The comments are not in order of priority or importance:

> Workload too heavy; lack of forward planning to spread this.
> Poor interpersonal relationships at work.
> Conflicting demands made by having different roles/responsibilities in different areas.
> Lack of feedback concerning points raised in discussions/decisions taken by management (any level of management).
> Too many meetings with too little structure, overloaded agenda, insufficient prior information/documentation.
> Too much administration, not sufficiently spread out.
> Students with personal difficulties who rely on staff to advise them when staff have little or no training in this area.
> General lack of clarity concerning tutorial role.
> Impact of Education Act, all the other new initiatives such as LMS, opting out, GCSEs, etc.
> Poor amount of INSET both within the working day and professionally organized for all who are interested (rather than the 'cascade' theory).
> Lack of sufficient non-contact time for preparation, marking, and discharging of other responsibilities.
> Lack of proper resources to do the job more efficiently or even properly.
> Financial problems.
> Lack of clerical assistance in the matter of exams, worksheets, duplicating, etc.
> No/little positive recognition of when a job is being done well under very trying circumstances.

A specific example of the effects of ineffective communications was given by one colleague:

Being moved out of your own teaching room for various reasons: Governors' meal, music adviser wants to teach in it, voting day, somebody's whim and being informed about it but not given an alternative room. You, thirty-one children, appropriate sets of books in bulging carrier bags, walking corridors in search of an empty space.

These teachers also reported difficult staff relationships as major organizational pressures. Some of the difficulties are identified in the following statements, which are quoted from my interviews:

There are new situations requiring new skills and attitudes but some members of staff suffer from an inability or an unwillingness to change.

Staff who are inexperienced, inadequate, poorly trained or simply unprofessional are an obvious burden to their more competent colleagues.

Some teachers here occasionally lack sensitivity or have insufficient knowledge of the individual child, thus creating potentially explosive situations arising out of relatively trivial incidents.

Newly qualified members of staff are often ill-equipped in teaching the basic skills. They become cynical or disillusioned when faced with the reality of the teaching situations. Weaknesses, doubts and feelings of guilt about performance are often repressed.

The occasions when fellow members of staff prove unreliable lead to pressure, since one is never quite certain whether one will be let down again.

There is a lack of interpersonal relationships, usually due to differences of opinions towards solutions to problems, e.g. pupil misbehaviour.

The next source of organizational stress to be discussed occurs more frequently in my reports than either poor communications or difficult staff relationships. This consists of heavy work loads, which in conjunction with inadequate time to complete them create the characteristic pressure situation of attempting to do more work in less time. When this situation is compounded by teachers concluding that there is a lack of recognition, appreciation and understanding of their increased effort, their feelings of frustration are heightened. These problems have been described as the 'avalanche effect' (endless bombardment with different classes); the 'treadmill effect' (because of the never-ending sequence of classes); or simply the 'conveyor belt effect' because of the timetable which requires staff to put on six to eight performances daily to a wide variety of audiences.

There is another aspect of the workload/time factor which needs to be considered. The problem is not only that teachers may not be able to complete all the tasks they are given or have set for themselves. It is also a question of not being able to achieve a level of performance in important aspects of their work which would bring good, warm feelings of a job well done. The feelings which are generated when teachers have not been able to do their work as well as they think it should be done are clearly identified in a report from a secondary school teacher:

> The response to these situations is a guilty feeling nearly all the time that nothing has been done properly and when I do try to relax I feel that I should be doing something in the way of preparation. This even applies during the holidays. Since starting teaching I have never been able to feel that everything has been completed satisfactorily and that I am properly prepared. There are many long-term projects on which I would like to spend time, but they are constantly shelved because there are more pressing and immediate demands.

The pressures and feelings which are referred to here are, I think, intensified by the perception that the time and effort which could be given to important tasks is being wasted on matters which are unimportant and probably useless. These are non-teaching activities: interruptions, telephone calls, paperwork and meetings which seem fruitless because nothing seems resolved after hours of discussion or because the significant decisions are taken by the head or senior management team. There are also frequent complaints about the time spent (and wasted) on pastoral and tutorial duties. One teacher summarized these concerns after they had been expressed by one of the working parties in an INSET conference:

> The organization should rethink its planning of the year and recognize that certain times are particularly stressful. Perhaps the timing of exams and reports should be rethought. Does the school need to have so many meetings? Although much of the pressure is externally initiated (National Curriculum), staff felt that the expectations of their managers were unrealistic (i.e. they wouldn't be able to re-write the whole of the 7 – 9 year courses for next year). Staff felt that their priorities ought to be teaching the pupils, marking and preparing lessons – but this seemed to be forgotten when they were being asked to revamp the whole of the curriculum, write and read policy documents on, for instance, staff management, concentrate on IDP, have INSET on primary/

secondary liaison and discuss the LEA's smoking policy at year meetings – all valuable and worthwhile, but putting teachers' energy elsewhere than in the classroom.

Therefore the organization should show their appreciation of good classroom practice by praising individuals and rewarding them (i.e. giving time for lesson preparation). The importance of classroom teaching should be self-evident.

The issues of meetings and decision-making without consultation discussed in this report are important aspects of another source of organizational stress caused by poor working conditions: the leadership of headteachers. The consequences for staff of heads' styles of leadership are important because of the power in the role to make significant decisions about pupils and teachers. This influence and the different ways it is used are still crucial factors in the attitudes, experience and expectations of staff. My reports suggest support for the view that heads' actions may increase staff stress and may make the school a place of frustration, anxiety, anger, threat and fear. Characteristics of the head reported to cause difficulties for staff include: autocratic leadership behaviour which ignores consultation and refuses to delegate decision-making and authority; indecisive or ambiguous leadership behaviour which does not provide clear and helpful guidelines for teachers; and unpredictability or inconsistency, which generates staff uncertainty and insecurity.

One of the experienced teachers on my Bristol courses was working in a secondary school whose head's style of leadership presented several of these aspects. The teacher was in a good position to observe this behaviour and its effects on her colleagues. She noted the disruptive style:

Today I feel we should have our Friday's Assembly even though it is only Thursday.

and the effect on staff:

Such changes mean many teachers' lesson plans are greatly disrupted, which when dealing with a difficult class asks for disaster. I have seen some of my colleagues' faces turn green with anger, frustration and the feeling of another bad start. Another trait of my present head teacher is her constant change of mood. One must take the day's temperature via the head's secretary before making any move towards the head's office. Permission to attend a course could for example be at stake.

Another kind of leadership behaviour which generates staff frustration is indecisiveness or ambiguity. It also causes confusion, conflict and much wasted effort. A clear indication of this problem was provided by the deputy head of a primary school:

> My main source of stress is the inconsistent nature of the headteacher. His inability to make decisions and abide by them means that the staff, and myself in particular, never know quite where we are. Accompanying this, he will not delegate completely but always checks and changes any work undertaken. This does create stress situations with myself and other members of staff. At present the only way one can deal with this is to try to forget school in one's own time.

The reluctance to make decisions which causes frustration and worry for staff is not restricted to the head. The pressures on staff are also caused by the action of the senior management team as they interact with heads of departments, heads of year, heads of house and staff. The focus of teachers' requests for decisions from heads and deputies is frequently the pupils' behaviour and some of the strongest and loudest demands are concerned with disruptive children. When the senior staff are indecisive in these circumstances – when they say they need to consult with social workers or probation officers before coming to a decision – the junior staff concerned feel a lack of support at a critical time which they resent. A teacher interviewed during a study of disruptive pupils in Sheffield (Galloway *et al.* 1982) gave a vivid description of incidents which had persuaded her that there was no point in seeking help because none would be given. She told her interviewer:

> Quite honestly, I tend not to refer kids for disruptive behaviour (to senior staff) if I can help it. It involves me in more hassles than it's worth. There's no trust in the relationships involved [i.e. between the speaker and her senior colleagues]. A number of kids have been put in the special group for disruptive pupils or have been sent out of school for swearing at the deputy – but if it is one of us it happens to, nothing is done. When I informed the head of a boy being rude to the school nurse, nothing was done. When he saw a similar incident several months later, the boy was excluded at once.

A similar problem was raised by a teacher in one of my interviews: 'I felt very little support when dealing with major discipline problems – including assault.'

These teachers would have been glad of the support of decisive actions by head and senior staff, but my reports also suggest that there are many occasions in school when teachers are not helped by their head's decisive behaviour if it is also autocratic. This kind of behaviour has a number of manifestations, which include refusing to delegate decision-making and authority, often because of the claim that the head has ultimate responsibility which cannot be shared. This style of leadership also relies only minimally on consultation and emphasizes the importance of what has been called 'initiating structure', in which the head defines the roles expected of each teacher by, for example, writing their job descriptions; establishes the aims of the school and promotes policies which in the head's opinion are necessary to achieve these goals. The autocrat pays little attention to 'consideration', which is respect and concern for the individual needs and interests of the members of staff.

Some of the negative aspects of autocratic behaviour have been identified by the teachers in my groups. From the closeness of a deputy's position in a comprehensive school an experienced teacher observed his head's behaviour:

> After a period of time attempting to put forward my own ideas without success and discovering that an unpleasant scene could arise from any initiative action which had not been given his minute scrutiny, one tended to fulfil one's administrative function mechanically and competently and concentrate on the teaching aspects of one's career, which was a negative solution. One felt resentful of being excluded and not gaining essential experience. In retrospect I wonder if I should have persisted in my own viewpoint in the initial stages of this post, but whereas this may work with tact and diplomacy with some heads, I do not consider in this case it would.

The organizational pressures and the financial and physical problems which were discussed earlier in this chapter may occur simultaneously and make a school an unhealthy workplace for members of staff. But, as the next chapter attempts to show, schools can also be sources of heavy pressures for the top management team.

7

PRESSURES ON THE SENIOR
MANAGEMENT TEAM

The last chapter was concerned with the pressures exerted by heads and deputies on members of staff. In the present chapter I shall be discussing the demands experienced by the senior management team. Teachers may be unaware of these problems and their criticisms of the leadership behaviour of senior management are, in my experience, often based upon a surprising degree of ignorance of the pressures exerted on them. Pressures from the media focus on the head and are increasing. Legal requirements have become more complex recently and the increase in administrative paperwork is described in heads' reports to me as a major burden. Increased expectations for accountability have already led to the introduction of time-consuming staff review procedures. The tasks of headship, for which heads are often untrained, include elements of negotiating, controlling, directing, punishing, accounting, planning, counselling, healing and reviewing.

The tasks involved in the deputy head's role are very difficult to catalogue in this way because the range of expectations varies so much from school to school. At one end of this range is a structured role description which is exemplified as Deputy Head (Curriculum) or Deputy Head (Pastoral). At the other end there may only be a vague job description where the role approximates to that of a personal assistant to an executive. If this role ambiguity follows a period of experiencing structure and reasonable clarity of aims as a head of department, the adjustment required to be effective in the deputy head's role is considerable. It may be only poorly appreciated by the staff, who may have little time or enthusiasm to be concerned with the problems of the top management team.

The identification of these and other pressures on senior staff is a major task of this chapter, and I want to start with the sources of work stress for heads.

PRESSURES ON HEADTEACHERS

There are a number of reports to substantiate their claim of increasing demands. A detailed analysis has been presented by Jenkins (1989):

Heads are faced with mounting pressures in managing their schools effectively as Government demands on education grow daily. The introduction of local management of schools with devolved financial powers and a new role for the governing body; the possibility of opting out; the bringing in of a national curriculum, pupil testing and new examinations; parental choice of schools; the creation of close links between school and industry; performance evaluation and teacher appraisal; all are manifest indicators of a formidable array of managerial tasks facing the head. Less obvious, however, but equally powerful, are the demands to raise standards in schools and to create in them, with the help of the Training Commission, a spirit of enterprise. All these demands, against the usual background of uncertainty about levels of finance, a growing shortage of teachers in key areas of the curriculum and low teacher morale, do appear overwhelming.

It should be noted however that these mounting pressures are additional to those already being exerted from different sources. They are not replacements. This point was well made by one of my respondents:

When one is a new head one expects worries and problems but, as time goes on, it is assumed that the job becomes slightly easier as experience comes to one's aid. Unfortunately this is not so. I find increasing pressures from the Authority (mainly because of continuing new legislation), constant changes in the curriculum and the ever-present demand to meet more and more deadlines. All these are additional to the pressures which have always been part of the job, e.g. standards, discipline, being the 'buffer' between staff and parents at times, child conduct, safety, etc. In other words, overall responsibility for all that goes on in school. One of the problems dealing with stress is trying to 'switch off' out of school. I try not to take work home with me and I live well away from the school and town. Worries are not too easy to leave behind.

Other headteachers report that they feel stress when things are getting on top of them because little hassles which individually could be tackled effectively occur simultaneously to form a crisis. For heads of primary schools these crises might be the result of a number of events occurring during the same day such as absent staff; teachers who for various reasons are unable to cope; children with behaviour problems which need urgent attention; parents with urgent complaints; a breakdown in supplies (for example heating or food) and teaching commitments. The headmaster of a secondary school gave an example of difficult situations which occurred simultaneously: a wet lunchtime in school exam week; a difficult parent arriving to see the head; a caretaker angry because of what happened in the previous night's disco; a bus strike during external examinations; a fire alarm test; a defunct boiler in the staffroom; lack of ventilation in overflowing toilets and teaching commitments.

The behaviour of parents is a source of pressure for heads in a number of ways. They report that they spend a disproportionate amount of time dealing with parents whose children are in conflict with one another. The head of a primary school gave me an example of this kind of problem:

> At a time when pupil violence against teachers is receiving much publicity, I am grateful to be able to report that this is not a stress with which I am faced. However, I would say that violence between children, is on occasion, one of the most worrying aspects of the modern school and I have been involved in dealing with such incidents. Some children just seem incapable of realizing the harm that they could do to others. We have had incidents that included the spiteful throwing of stones, attempted strangling, biting and kicking. Fortunately in the majority of cases the parents have been helpful in backing the school, but in some unfortunate cases the parents have been singularly unhelpful and positively antagonistic towards the staff. There was one incident in which teachers saw an incident involving kicking, but the parents refused to accept the situation and accused the teachers of lying and having a vendetta against their child. This was, in fact, dealt with by direct confrontation with the parents and the sheer weight of evidence. In another incident where a child had attacked another the teacher on duty had to haul the attacker off and was unfortunately injured in the process. Treatment is still going on. The procedure now is that in the event of such a happening, my presence is immediately called for in the playground. I can't say this bothers me too much as the incidents are relatively infrequent but there is always the nagging concern that perhaps something could go drastically wrong.

Parental pressures also evoke other strong emotions, for example, when schools are in multi-ethnic and disadvantaged inner-city areas. The parents of children in these schools may have enormous problems and when they come into school they often seek help from the headteacher or deputy head. When the help which can be offered is inadequate, heads and deputies may experience feelings of anxiety, helplessness and depression. The children's problems are major sources of stress for two reasons. Heads want to give support to a teacher who is finding the classroom situation very difficult to manage and they become directly involved in helping the children. Outside agencies which include social services, police, Department of Health and Social Security officials and probation officers have responsibilities for these families and the workloads of headteachers and deputy heads are increased by trying to overcome barriers to effective inter-professional communications with them. If there is a sense of failure because little has been achieved and if there is a sense of guilt at the amount of time spent on one child's problems, the stress factor is increased.

Parental pressure is also felt as a result of their increasing expectations of playing a greater part in the work and management of the school. These changing expectations, which have greatly increased since the Reform Act, have led to more questions being asked by parents about the aims and facilities of the school. The head of a primary school suggested an additional explanation for these increasing demands: 'Parents are now thoroughly upset by the media and particularly by the reports of "a lack of basics" in school.'

Pressures from parents and pressures from the media are becoming more closely related. Articles published in the press have presented parents with lists of questions to ask heads. The use of these lists has resulted in demands for information about heads' qualifications and educational values and even the state of the toilets.

A different but still difficult media pressure was reported by the head of a comprehensive school:

> The public criticism in the local newspaper two years ago caused a great deal of stress for my staff and myself. It arose through the appointment as a governor of the school a parent who had transferred his child to another school. This was reported with some derogatory comments by the paper and was followed by several weeks of letters for and against the school, encouraged by the paper. I was in fact away on a year's secondment at the time, but I reacted very strongly with a mixture of intense anger and anxiety, as did many of the staff – perhaps because of our helplessness to do anything about it.

Those media comments on education which demand higher standards of pupil achievement and teacher performance have additional consequences. One of the most significant is that teachers feel undervalued by their local community and the country as a whole.

These feelings of being undervalued are, I think, reinforced by the contraction in the Education Service. One important aspect is the

71

restricted allowance allocated to schools, which, as the Schools Inspectorate reported in 1990, has resulted in one-quarter of state comprehensive and grammar schools suffering from serious shortages of even basic equipment such as electrical meters, microscopes and electronic kits. The effect of contraction in primary schools was indicated by a survey of 129 primary heads conducted by the National Association of Head Teachers in 1990. Over one-third were having to make cuts to their equipment and books budget to make ends meet.

Contraction has also resulted in the reduction of staff in schools because of falling rolls. One major consequence in primary schools has been the acceptance by the head of the responsibilities of full-time class teacher. The implications of this change are clearly outlined by the head of an infant school:

> This Infant School has been reduced in number from 278 to 79, i.e. a reduction from ten full-time staff to three. The cuts in teaching staff caused me to decide to teach a class full-time. The problems caused by my teaching commitment are:
> 1 Lack of contact with parents, who normally are welcome to call any time.
> 2 Interruption, causing the disruption of my class and a lack of continuity in my teaching.
> 3 Inability to teach other classes and get to know the children.
> 4 Inability to visit other classes while the teacher and children are working.
> 5 Difficulty in discussing problems with staff because of lack of time in catching up with administration, messages, telephone calls, etc.
> 6 Not enough time to give visiting students in-service training, etc.
> 7 Stress of constantly being aware of areas which need attention and yet being unable through lack of time, energy or the demands of one's class to deal with them.
> 8 Various problems have also been caused by the deterioration in the standard of repairs of the building, which is over 100 years old, and the increase in administrative work required. However the reductions in staffing and the necessity to teach full-time have caused greater problems.
> I have had more absence from school during the last year than at any time for six years. I have had influenza, laryngitis, whooping cough and cervical spondylosis.

The problems of the head who teaches full time are also vividly presented in the following report:

With particular reference to a very small village school headteacher in complete charge of a class (small part-time relief). A one room situation. Stresses can develop from the following and as a result of:

1 The loneliness of the situation. Lack of adult conversation, companionship and stimulation.
2 Being in the same 'one room' environment throughout the day (no staffroom or any other room).
3 Complete lack of privacy.
4 Decisions to be made without consultations with deputy head or other staff.
5 No protection from 'invasion' – belligerent parents or any other visitors.
6 No other adult present to act as witness or in support of actions or statements made.
7 All correspondence – accounts, forms, letters to be made with children present.
8 Auxiliary and support services (doctor, dentist, educational psychologist) – all visits and discussions must necessarily be made with children present.
9 Telephone calls in and out from school to be made in the same room. Constant interruptions from children make telephone conversations difficult.
10 Complete charge of children throughout the day in one environment – dinners served and eaten (also supervised).

To sum up – A very lonely, isolated, vunerable situation.

Contraction has also meant reduced opportunities for personal and professional growth. Appointment to a headship would usually be associated with expectations of change and progress, not with decline. But the following report from the head of a middle school shows how great was the difference between optimistic anticipation and harsh experience;

> The cuts in educational spending started just as I became a head, so my time was spent preserving existing ideas and standards rather than being creative and expanding educational ideas. Staff cuts meant a lack of flexibility so that a minor crisis had a knock-on effect and disrupted many plans. The long-term plans kept having to be scrapped because the cuts were never known about until the last moment. The County did not appear to have any concern for the welfare of new heads.

Similar comments have been made by other heads about the behaviour of their LEA officials. They claim that in dealing with their Authority they have had to be very patient and must be prepared to accept that what they consider to be urgent for their school will not receive the attention by the County officials which the situation requires. The head of a primary school gave further details of these problems:

> I feel that a lot of stress is caused by requests to County Hall not being dealt with promptly, no acknowledgement of requests or reasons for delay, thus incurring too many unnecessary letters and telephone calls to chase up things which should have been dealt with without any reminder being necessary. The school governors, the PTA and myself have been fighting for the provision of an extra temporary classroom for the last two years, when it was first promised. Class 2 teacher's stress was relieved when the new classroom came into use at the beginning of this term. If the classroom had been erected a year earlier, life would have been less stressful for that classteacher and myself, as apart from the interruptions caused by the delay and the erection of the classroom we were both 'bulging at the seams' as far as numbers were concerned.

The increase in pressure caused by changes in the headteacher's role is emphasized in a report from NFER with the intriguing title 'Keeping the Raft Afloat' (Earley *et al.* 1990). This is a study of 204 heads appointed to their first headships in 1982-3. Eighty per cent of them claimed that their role now was very difficult when compared with their first headship. The four major changes were:

- Responding to LEA and government initiatives
- Becoming managers or administrators
- Dealing with public relations and promoting the school's image
- Supporting or protecting staff.

These demands, which have greatly increased as a result of a wide range of reforms introduced by the 1986 and 1988 Education Acts, are directly related to 'the growing evidence of stress among existing senior managers, the rapid rate of retirement and the falling off of the numbers of those applying for headships and deputy headships'. (Styan 1989:B29).

One of the heaviest costs of the new initiatives reported by heads has been a large increase in paperwork. The head of a middle school wrote:

> I have just received another package of bureaucracy from the Department of Education and Science. This time it's ten copies of the annual curriculum return (ACR), three copies of the new set of statutory regulations concerning it and three copies of a letter explaining the revised form of the return. This lot, with the

plethora of information/advice requirements arriving on my desk from other bodies such as the National Curriculum Council, the School Examinations and Assessment Council and the local authority must account for at least three Amazonian rainforest trees, sent to the school this academic year.

(Hall 1990:19)

Many of the heads in the NFER research (Earley *et al.* 1990) regretted the role change from 'leading professional' to 'chief executive' which had been caused by several of the initiatives but particularly LMS (Local Management of Schools). They were also anxious about this change because they did not feel they had the necessary skills to carry out their management responsibilities under the Reform Act or that they would receive adequate training and support.

The experience of heads before and after the introduction of LMS on 1 April 1990 suggests that these apprehensions were fully justified. There is a growing awareness that the human implications of this change are much wider than balancing a balance sheet. There are, for instance, much greater civil and criminal liabilities of heads and governors. These are specified in a new guide to employment and industrial relations law for headteachers which was compiled for the National Association of Headteachers by Greville Janner QC, a specialist in employment law (1989).

But it is the experience of formula funding which is causing so much anxiety and anger, because as one very experienced head has written so clearly:

No planning could have foreseen the consequences of formula funding for any individual school. Everyone knew there would be winners and losers without knowing where or how. The early chaos seems to be showing plenty of losers but few winners.

(Vaughan 1990:25)

The losers have to try to balance reduced funding with increased expenditure because of staff salary increases and inflation. Even with income generation this head believes:

Schools will simply not be able to afford what they have now. My dilemma is shared by colleagues not only in my own authority but in other areas. Regrettably there is only one place to economise and be able to sleep at night. Teachers' costs make up 76 per cent of my delegated total. Fortunately a young able member of staff is leaving in August to get married so I do not face the trauma of recommending a redundancy to my governors. The school will have to be organised with one teacher less.

(Vaughan 1990:25)

It is partly because of this rigid requirement of balancing the budget that 'heads resent the new pressures on them to compete for customers and spend time and money on the business of improving their image'. (Finch 1990). The pressure to do so is widespread and appears to be irresistible. According to a survey published in 1990 by Tim Devlin Enterprises, a schools public relations consultancy, thirty-seven LEAs were encouraging schools to appoint media press officers and sixty schools had positively responded in twenty-five authorities. The Industrial Society has organized well attended seminars for heads and deputies to discuss the skills of marketing. The National Association of Headteachers issued guidelines in 1990 on how heads should and should not market their schools. Gifts and 'commercial incentives' were banned, as were 'comparisons or statements which denigrate other schools'.

Heads feel that they must take part in these competitive marketing activities or their schools will not survive in a free market for customers, though some of them are 'deeply sceptical' (Sutcliffe 1989) of the educational value of what they are doing and the jargon involved (for example USP or Unique Selling Point). Other heads are much more enthusiastic about these marketing initiatives because they believe that there are many good things in state education that people never hear about, that marketing skills can help schools to improve their communications with the public and perhaps begin to change the derogatory images which many members of the public appear to have about schools and teachers, and that marketing can be a co-operative enterprise as secondary heads in Avon and Essex are demonstrating.

There are other important human implications of the initiatives of the Reform Act which are bringing pressures on headteachers. The following list of the major pressures on a group of twenty-four heads of first and middle schools shows the 'knock-on' effect of these changes. Their major pressures reported to me were:

- Staff
- Constant demands on time and energy from others
- Conflict between what brings enjoyable job satisfaction and what is mundane but necessary
- Conflict between time to do what is important and time to do what is urgent
- Tremendous changes which are taking place
- Vast quantities of paper and guidelines which have to be read and interpreted to confused staff
- Lack of time to listen to staff about their problems and difficulties
- Administration
- Difficult and assertive people.

These heads gave me details of the behaviour and attitudes of staff which were causing them considerable difficulties. Four major problems were identified. These were:

- Incompetent/weak members of staff who need and are given much help and encouragement but do not develop the skills they lack.
- Unadaptable staff whose resistance to all innovations in school whether concerned with induction, appraisal, INSET, initiatives from the Reform Act, length of the school day or changes in staffroom furniture takes the form of non-involvement, isolation from colleagues or cynicism.
- Disappointed staff who have not achieved the career goals they set themselves in the early years of their experience in an expanding Education Service. As several reports from staff suggest they may feel 'trapped at 40' with little or no realistic prospects of promotion and feelings of alienation from the values they see in the new business culture of their school.
- Stressed staff who have been unable to assimilate all the initiatives of the Reform Act, which represent for some colleagues a culture shock with significant personal, professional, organizational and family consequences. The signs of stress which are now being reported by many research workers are often happening for the first time to staff without the opportunity of developing the necessary coping strategies or even the possibility of adequate preparation for new pressures.

These difficulties are major concerns for these headteachers, who also identified another important source of stress. This was their own very high levels of self-expectation. A head of a primary school identified this problem for herself and her colleagues:

> There is an overwhelming pressure caused by an over-expectation of one's own abilities – trying to be all things to all people. These self-induced pressures are also caused by being constantly aware one should be doing more, especially in curriculum planning, innovation, support for weak or inexperienced teachers, etc., etc.

But there are headteachers with a very different approach to their jobs. A much more relaxed and 'B type' perspective was provided for a workshop by the Principal of a sixth-form college:

> Thank you for your letter. On reading it I decided that my problems regarding stress are probably the reverse of most people's. The pace of life here is such that the only people who experience stress are those who come in from outside and try to accelerate matters!

77

My staff have all been redeployed to the college from local schools in which innovation, in terms of teaching methods, curriculum development and pastoral care, had been conspicuous by its absence in the main. The schools were all run with the termly or half-termly staff meeting as the only forum for discussion and advancement.

As most of the staff are in their 40s and 50s it has not been easy to alter this approach. Gradually such things as department meetings, working parties, and planning meetings are beginning to develop after 18 months and attaining a grudging acceptance as part of the job! However we are several years (if not light years!) away from any kind of staff stress!

On the credit side the members of staff are very pleasant, sane people who enjoy their jobs and have other balancing interests and responsibilities. I find it quite re-assuring in a way when senior heads of department miss meetings to visit an elderly parent or watch City in a cup replay.

In my experience this attitude is rather rare. I am more likely to find heads exposed to heavy external pressures who also subject themselves to very high and perhaps unrealistic expectations of their own performance and that of their colleagues. They are putting themselves (and their colleagues) at risk of developing and perhaps exacerbating stress reactions. These include guilt and anxiety and frustration, but they also are characterized by poor relationships at school and at home. At school, staff suffer from the head under stress. But often it is the deputy who is particularly vulnerable, and difficult relationships with the head are one of the deputy's major work pressures.

PRESSURES ON DEPUTY HEADS

These pressures can be divided into three main groups (Knutton and Mycroft 1986):

1 A wide range of responsibilities
2 Role Conflict
3 Difficult relationships with head, staff, pupils and parents.

There is a wide range of tasks in the role of deputy, from the very trivial to the very important. There are urgent, unplanned situations requiring instant attention, for example a parent or a pupil or a colleague in distress. The range of work for some deputies includes coping with staff absences; trying to improve the performance of poor teachers and motivating those who are running out of hope of promotion; controlling disruptive pupils and trying to motivate those

78

pupils, who because of a high incidence of unemployment in the catchment area of the school believe that school achievement is irrelevant to their future; and teaching a considerable number of lessons on a regular basis. The extensive and elastic nature of the role is perhaps best seen when there is no job description and the deputy is told by the head that the development of the job is dependent on his or her personality, experience and skills. But the existence of a job description is no guarantee that the post-holder will have an accurate perception of the boundaries of the job. There are extension clauses built into job descriptions as the following example from a deputy in a secondary school illustrates:

The official version of my job description when appointed is shown below:

Oversight and co-ordination of the administration of the school.

Preparation of the timetable.

Arrange for staff cover.

Staff duties and staff welfare.

Oversight of the pastoral care structure in the school.

Production of the monthly staff circular and the minutes of the various year heads' and department heads' meetings.

Membership of several school and PTA committees.

Responsibility for in-service training and for probationary teachers.

Press liaison and general public relations.

School discipline.

The job description also included the statement:

The list is intended to be no more than a guide to the deputy's duties. The successful candidate must have the necessary ability and energy to become involved in all aspects of the school and to make a significant contribution to its continued development.

A number of problems are associated with this wide range of expectations. Role conflict is one of the most serious and frequent. There are different kinds of conflict situations which put pressures on deputies. One type occurs when the deputy has a major teaching commitment, as in the following report:

My dual role as teacher and administrator causes stress. I teach a half timetable and I find that my lessons are often interrupted by office staff and also by colleagues, who either come themselves with problems or send pupils to me when they feel that they cannot deal with them. I take my teaching seriously and I am very conscious of my duty to my pupils and my need to set a good example to my colleagues. I appreciate, on the other hand, that the teacher with a full timetable meets situations which need to be 'cooled down' immediately and that he feels his need is great. Some of the interruptions are obviously concerned with trivia; others, although at first appearing to be minor, have turned out to be serious.

Strong pressure also occurs for deputies when they attempt to reconcile conflicting interests in school, which include those between pupil and pupil; between pupil and teacher; between teachers themselves; between members of staff and the head and between staff and parents.

There are conflicting interests between 'today' and 'tomorrow', that is, between the demands of day-to-day work and the need for long-term planning. There is a similar conflict between the unpredictable crises of staff and pupils and the deputy's own daily list of priorities. These problems often result in the major time pressures which are identified in my reports. One woman who said she was under severe stress wrote:

> I am literally pursued along corridors by staff. I have no breaks or lunch hour. My dinner consumption has been timed at 2 minutes 38 seconds by a colleague.

Conflict is reported because of uncertainty about other people's roles in the school and confusion about their areas of responsibility. This situation leads to considerable frustration and anxiety when the role of the deputy head is undefined in a school and role boundaries are unclear between members of the senior management team or between them and middle management.

Some of these problems are met because of the differences between expectations and experience which are often greatest for newly appointed deputies. I can illustrate these difficulties by presenting the pre-workshop report of a vice-principal who had been three months in post:

> I do feel that there *is* a real and vast difference between middle and senior management and, no matter how friendly the staff are – and ours *are* that – there is still a strong sense of 'us' (i.e. the staff) and 'them' (i.e. principal and vice-principals). I think I have been 'caught out' on one or two occasions in seeking the security of 'us' again; I clearly left this one behind with my previous job though I did not expect to.
>
> The staff generally have a positive attitude towards management but I feel compelled by what I think are their perceptions into being what I thought I would avoid like the plague: a vice-principal first and a member of staff second. I remember strongly

a casual remark by one of the senior staff: 'Of course people will only tell you what they want you to know.' I think this is an excellent description of my situation in my new role and, pleasant though my present situation is, it's difficult to find adequate feedback at times.

Relationship problems with colleagues have also been reported to me by deputies in other types of schools. One of my respondents – a deputy in a primary school – encountered difficulties with her headteacher and members of staff:

> I took over as a deputy head well aware of the problems I was to face. I had been warned by colleagues and advisers that the head was an autocrat. This proved to be very true. As soon as I tried to make any decisions I was firmly put in my place. I also felt that certain members of staff were hostile as they had wanted my post. The pressures were increased by the fact that the previous deputy had been a great friend of the head and was still brought back to take part in concerts and go on school journeys, all of which made me feel rather inadequate. The symptoms of stress took the form of severe headaches and I became very short tempered at home, especially with my own children.

Some of the relationship difficulties which deputies (and headteachers) discuss in my workshops are related to the task of counselling staff. Some colleagues want a sounding board for their professional and personal problems; others request a critical appraisal of their career prospects; a few need to cry and more want to complain; a number seek advice on job applications and interviews and courses; a growing number seek help with stress management and leaving the profession. The weight of these demands was clearly expressed by a deputy in a secondary school:

> The most stressful situations are those where I am called upon to resolve stress or conflict in other people's relationships. Having said that, it is important to add I find this to be one of the more interesting and challenging elements of the job as well as that which generates most stress.

The frustration and resentment which can be generated by these demands when they are not seen as challenging and interesting can be felt in the report of a deputy head:

> My pressures include having to cope with problems beyond the scope of my training. I am not a psychologist, nor a psychiatrist, nor a social worker, nor a marriage guidance counsellor.

This is a common complaint and it may indicate an unwillingness to become involved in the development of pastoral care for teachers. This attitude of members of the senior management team has important implications for all members of staff because it limits the range of alternative sources of help which are available in school. But my work with heads of departments and pastoral care team leaders suggests that these members of middle management are urgently in need of the support of top management because of the problems they experience. Their pressures are identified in the next chapter.

8

PRESSURES ON MIDDLE MANAGEMENT

The first part of this chapter is concerned with the demands generated by substantial changes in the role of head of department. One major change has resulted in departmental heads becoming involved in management responsibilities for the work of the staff in their departments while still being required to carry a heavy teaching programme. The second part of the chapter discusses the pressures on pastoral care heads arising from their wide range of duties, which includes being responsible for pupils' discipline, pupils' problems and liaison with external agencies as well as having to teach for much of the week. Heads of houses and heads of year are also experiencing increased levels of stress themselves but they also have to cope with the stress being felt by their colleagues.

PRESSURES ON HEADS OF DEPARTMENT

The change in the role of departmental heads is an important area for investigation. There used to be a sharp contrast between holding the post in a grammar or a comprehensive school. Formerly the managerial aspects of a head of department's role in a grammar school often involved little more than ordering books for the department once a year. But now, in the 1990s, curricular and organizational changes are affecting both types of secondary school. Heads of departments in grammar schools are experiencing pressures similar to those being exerted on their comprehensive-school colleagues. The person in the post of departmental head now has an amplified role in which extra duties and responsibilities have to be fitted into a full teaching schedule. There is very little provision made in school time for the very many jobs connected with the management of a department. The resulting loss of effectiveness can be considerable.

Several types of demands which have resulted from these curricular and organizational changes can be identified in the following report by a head of department in a grammar school:

> During this academic year we have been faced with tremendous reorganization plans in an attempt to implement the National Curriculum and keep the range of subjects, particularly Classics, available to pupils. Heads of department for the first time have found themselves fighting for their subjects, trying to deal with overmanning in certain departments, having to devise new courses and find new resources. Their role has completely changed. In addition they have also had to deal with their department's anxiety about the prospect of a nine-period day from next September and the implications of this for part-time and full-time colleagues. The lack of consultation and discussion by senior management has added to the frustration felt by many middle managers and this is highlighted by the large number who seriously consider leaving teaching. In fact the head of Mathematics decided to take early retirement as his way of coping with the stress resulting from this reorganisation.

Other effects of these changes were reported by another head of department:

> I think that the spontaneity of classroom relationships – the fun – has been displaced by tight organization, targets, appraisal, reports, parental pressure and expectations of teachers.

These reports suggest that increased administrative responsibilities are now an integral part of the role of head of department in secondary schools. But the management of a department has important relationship aspects and my informants indicate that interaction with colleagues can be a major source of stress. The difficult behaviour, indifferent attitudes and incompetence of staff create considerable problems for their head of department, particularly if there is a lack of time to keep a careful check on what every member of the department is teaching. Problems arise when a department is mainly composed of young, first- and second-year teachers who may need a lot of guidance, especially when most of them are tackling examination work for the first time. The members of the department who fail to pull their weight, who cannot keep good discipline in their classes, who have low academic and professional skills, or who are the subjects of complaints by pupils, parents and staff bring extra worry and work. Lack of initiative and ambition in some staff, their lack of co-operation, lack of effort and resistance to change are responsible for the development of considerable levels of frustration. There is also a problem of continuity when levels of staff turnover and absenteeism are high. Some of these problems of staff management can be recognized in the analysis by a head of department in a comprehensive school:

I was appointed to introduce Integrated Science across the ability ranges, revitalize a department much entrenched in traditional methods of teaching and reorganize the resources base. The job has been made more difficult because I only have one experienced teacher (out of five) who is committed with me to the introduction of Integrated Science. Consequently the workload has been taken on jointly by us and an MPG teacher who has been assisting with the preparation of suitable syllabuses, development of new resources pertinent to the new courses, etc.

In the last month my inexperienced MPG colleague, who nevertheless was giving her wholehearted support to me and the new direction of the department, announced that her husband had secured a job in South Africa and that she would be leaving a week before the end of the term. I have not managed to secure a replacement for next term on a temporary contract (to offer Physics to 'O' level) and the County refuse to allow a permanent post to be offered until redeployment procedures have been carried out. Where do I find time for myself and my colleague to undertake urgent curriculum development for September when we are covering a full timetable for a vacant post?

In addition to these problems I have had to learn the skills of mediation, diplomacy, balancing the books, coping with the decorators in for three weeks, etc., etc. There is more but you asked for this to be kept brief.

Role conflict occurs for the head of department as he or she acts as an intermediary with other departmental heads or with house or year heads. The head of department is required to act as a negotiator and this leads to feelings of vulnerability in 'boundary' situations where there is disagreement about the respective areas of responsibility. One said:

I find that other heads of department are very, very sensitive when they think that anyone else is encroaching on their department. Some of them are very set in their ways and refuse to recognize any form of change when discussions on curriculum development are held.

The head of department may also experience role conflict in opening or maintaining channels of communication between teachers in the department and the senior management team. Staff may want their departmental head to put their point of view to the head and deputies, or if they are inexperienced they may need reassurance when they communicate with members of the management team whom they see as authority figures.

Heads of departments experience other kinds of problems in their dealings with senior management. The leadership behaviour of head-teachers has been indicated by my informants as a major source of stress. Their reports suggest that serious difficulties are caused by several facets of heads' management styles including their reluctance to delegate any responsibility for decision-making, a lack of communication between them and their middle management, failure to appreciate the needs of individual departments which results in bad timetabling, failure to provide clear job descriptions for heads of departments and their colleagues, inability to provide a clear style of decision-making, the appointment of staff without departmental consultation, the introduction of significant curricular changes without the participation of the departmental head, making timetable changes for staff without reference to the department, and finally the 'whittling away' of a department because of the head's negative opinion about the importance of the subject.

The identification of these pressures caused by role conflict and increased administrative responsibilities provides strong, contemporary support for the conclusions of a headmaster who wrote an innovatory analysis of the effects of changes in the role of head of department twenty years ago:

> Leading a department in a large comprehensive school is, one must admit, very exhausting. The total number of hours involved and the total quantity of energy used are very high indeed. The sheer pressure of decisions required and initiatives to take will surprise the teacher who moves from a tripartite school system and often indeed the new appointment who has had previous experience in a less senior post in a comprehensive school. The priorities are difficult to establish and there is continuous tension in the head of department's task – arguably more than in the post of headteacher.
>
> (Marland 1971:98)

This analysis was important because it helped post-holders and those teachers who were intending to apply for these posts to develop an objective awareness of the changing characteristics of the head of department's job. My aim in this chapter has also been to provide an up-to-date review which would stimulate an awareness of the nature of departmental responsibilities, which have become more onerous because of the heavy volume of National Curriculum business. This includes for some colleagues very frequent meetings which are very pressurized because there is not enough time to deal with any item on the agenda properly.

PRESSURES ON PASTORAL CARE HEADS

In my discussion of he middle-management role of head of house or year, I wish to show that these appointments often carry very heavy pressures and if the people appointed are to meet these demands effectively the different components of their workload must be identified. My analysis suggests that the major problems are: multiplicity of tasks; too much work of a crisis management nature; a conflict between teaching responsibilities and pastoral care commitments; teamwork problems; poor communication with the senior management team, colleagues and outside agencies; role conflict because of contradictory expectations of pupils, staff and parents. The pressures arising from the multiplicity of tasks in the role were clearly noted by a very experienced senior tutor and head of third year. His report clearly identified the two major sources of stress in his work:

- unclear definition of role and number of roles
- conflicting priorities and pressure from outside.

I believe that the main source of stress in teaching lies in this area, when at one and the same time a number of 'immediate and urgent' category issues arise. To give one example from last week. The day began with the suggestion that one of the boys from Year 9 had tampered with bikes. That required immediate attention, including finding boys who were supposed witnesses. In the middle of interviewing them a member of Year 11, who was thought to be missing from school that day, turned up, not in school uniform, asking to see me urgently. It transpired that the previous night he had assaulted both parents, left his home and now didn't know what to do. That required immediate counselling and during that other issues came to light that were of a very serious nature. During this, two parents 'phoned the school with matters for my attention, both of which required me to follow up issues with boys. I also had to interview a boy whose family had just moved into the area from South Africa to see whether he will be suitable for our Year 9 or Year 10 next year. This obviously involved tests and talking to him. It was fortunate that of a six-period morning I was only teaching three periods, but these had to be done as well.

I do not believe that this is untypical of what can happen these days in schools, but the situation is not helped for those willing to be involved when we are expected to be police, social workers, careers teachers, teachers of morality, etc., expected to extend the curriculum, teach it all better, produce exam results, etc. and often assume the mantle of delegated parenthood. In something I had printed in The Times recently I claimed (and still hold) that these roles are taken on readily but what is lacking are the facilities (including time, recognition and support) to do the tasks properly. The greatest stress comes from the inability without virtual self-martyrdom to do all the various tasks as well as we feel we could and should for the sake of those in our care.

As this detailed self-appraisal of the crisis management and role conflict aspects of the pastoral care middle management role suggests, there is often insufficient time to deal with the problems that arise and the pastoral team head may experience feelings of guilt because of missing meetings or having to go late to lessons or perhaps missing them altogether when parents or outside agencies or children need his or her attention.

These significant demands were also revealed during my investigations with three National Association for Pastoral Care In Education (NAPCE) regional associations which had invited me to one of their meetings to discuss my work in helping teachers cope with stress. Before each of these meetings the secretary sent to the members a copy of the questionnaire I had prepared. It had four questions:

1 What are the pressures you experience as a result of your involvement in pastoral care in your school?
2 How do you try to cope with these pressures?
3 What are your reactions if these coping strategies are ineffective?
4 What recommendations have you for reducing the pressures on teachers involved in pastoral care?

Their replies to these questions suggest that my questionnaire provided teachers with the opportunity to express their feelings at length. Only a minority took advantage of this opportunity. Most of the NAPCE members who responded sent me one- or two-sentence answers. When the statements were compiled into a checklist they revealed many pressures which pastoral-care staff experience at work.

Checklist of pastoral work pressures on staff

1 Time pressures
2 Maintaining consistent priorities
3 Asked to do too many things
4 Dealing with and identifying other people's problems
5 Clearing up other teachers' discipline problems – especially when the kids are in the right

6 Not able to do anything about pupils' problems

7 Extra preparation – more so because content is unfamiliar

8 Need to use different teaching methods from those one is used to

9 Massive workload impinges on normal teaching and preparation

10 Staff expectations that you are the solver of all problems immediately

11 The knowledge of your limitations at the outset

12 When to delegate to tutors and when to 'chase' them

13 Need for job description as far as involving senior school management in decision-making

14 Lack of information

15 My preparation time for teaching is often hampered by pastoral problems

16 There are so many changes being suggested in relation to pastoral care

17 Wanting to respond to criticism honestly (e.g. from parents) but having to protect inadequate colleagues

18 Being faced by insolent (and at times idiot) teenagers and not having the real power to deal with them

19 Dealing with some kinds of teenagers on behalf of colleagues who have had altercations with kids who behave as if you were these staff

20 Inadequate resources

21 Lack of training

22 Contact with hostile parents

23 Having to be available at all times all day to children, parents, outside agencies

24 Continual listening to other people's problems, especially in a crisis

25 Too many problems to cope with properly

26 The pupils' home backgrounds do not change

27 Torn between responsibility to class and need to communicate with person/persons in need

28 Concern that a major problem may be overlooked

29 Tension between one's role as counsellor and one's role as link in disciplinary chain

30 Difficulty of establishing one-to-one relationship in a large group

A number of the statements refer specifically to the pressures directed towards responsibilities to tutors, for example 5, 10, 12, 13, 19 and 23. Some respondents used the opportunity of completing the questionnaire to write detailed and comprehensive analyses of their pastoral-care roles as a form of self-appraisal. An example of the latter is this report by a head of year, which indicates the wide range of role expectations he experienced:

The main pressure arises from the sheer range over which I operate including (a) formal duties, intensified by the members of staff who have opted out of lunchtime duties, (b) oversight of year curriculum and progress of pupils, (c) liaison with primary schools – this is currently a rapid growth area of work, (d) parental contacts covering a wide area of problems, (e) responsibility for fixtures/fittings in the year area, i.e. one-fifth of the school area, and its appearance, (f) contacts with Welfare Social Services relating to specific pupils, (g) staff leadership and development of a team of year staff, (h) the diversity of daily lunchtime and termly evening social activities, (i) the need to keep formal financial accounts for all activities – each year being self-financing, (j) oversight of the behaviour and discipline of all pupils within my year area for each period of the day, (k) dining hall supervision while the year are having lunch. Generally I have tried to group those aspects creating 'pressures' as shown above, but there may well be omissions – for example another which now occurs to me is the pressure of my teaching commitment, where traditionally the year head has the 'more awkward classes'.

My present school is now undergoing quite radical changes but previously a further problem was quite simply the lack of definite guidelines as to 'year head role'. The job was what one made it and brought great responsibility but always with uncertainty – one always knew a task had been taken too far when knuckles were rapped, regardless of any benefit which may have accrued to the school. To avoid this situation of 'responsibility without real authority' it became the custom for each year-head to operate in isolation and only communicate necessary information. As a result further pressure was created e.g. how do other year-heads deal with vandalism, bullying, spitting, religious assemblies, grafitti and so on.

This perceptive self-review expresses very clearly the twin demands of role conflict and time pressures which are constantly operating on pastoral heads.

The specific circumstances in school when these pressures are most demanding are often related to the severe problems of pupils and their families which the pastoral-care heads and tutors attempt to resolve by using many hours in listening, talking, telephoning social services and other outside agencies, convening case conferences and writing reports. This 'individual cases' time is given at the expense of time which is required for other activities, for example teaching. One report from a secondary school tutor gave me insight into these pressures in a vivid and harrowing manner:

I would be particularly grateful if the question of coping with bereavement of children in the group could be dealt with – I say this with great feeling, being a tutor in secondary school where a group is your responsibility for seven years. In the past eleven years three of my pupils have died and I am at present coming to terms with another pupil who has leukaemia. I am appalled by the insensitivity shown – I have been told of a pupil's death at 9.30 a.m. and expected to make an appearance in the classroom to teach at 9.35 a.m.! Any show of grief or shock seems to be taken as a sign of weakness and lack of ability to cope with the job.

This discussion of some of the heavy demands arising from the management of pastoral care in schools concludes this chapter on the problems found in middle-management roles (see also Dunham (1987)). It is also the end of the section of the book which identifies the sources of pressure on all levels of staff. The next chapter is concerned with the important dimension of teachers' reactions to these pressures.

9

IDENTIFICATION OF STRESS REACTIONS

In this chapter stress reactions to the pressures identified in the previous eight chapters will be grouped into four main types: behavioural, emotional, mental and physical.

These four kinds of reactions were recognized by the teachers referred to in the last chapter who were experiencing heavy pressures from their pastoral-care responsibilities. Their reports of behavioural reactions included:

Heavy smoking, driving too fast and an inability to sit still and relax.

A report of emotional signs of stress identified:

A general feeling that the workload is so heavy that it is impossible to cope. Much of the pastoral work makes me feel that I am wasting my time. Thinking about it causes depression.

A report of mental reactions noted:

Constant self-control is essential for me to establish my priorities and to stick to them. My judgment suffers by virtue of having too much 'on the plate' and so little available time to give full consideration to a problem.

Their recognition of physical symptoms incuded:

I have constant headaches and constriction around the windpipe due to tension. There is an inability to sleep properly because of an over-reactive mind at 3 a.m. When things get bad at the end of term I get indigestion and palpitations.

These types of reactions should be regarded as manifestations of stress because they indicate levels of pressure in excess of the teachers' coping resources. They can be identified in the following checklist compiled from the teachers' questionnaire statements:

Check list of reactions to stress

1 Over-sensitivity to criticism
2 Feelings of insecurity
3 Inappropriate responses to children
4 I react by feeling depressed about these pressures
5 Feeling of inadequacy
6 Lack of confidence
7 Becoming 'uptight'
8 Teachers make lessons over-structured and tense
9 Exhaustion
10 Short temper
11 Wake up during the night thinking of problems
12 Considerable reluctance to be involved in any sort of pastoral work
13 Frustration
14 Delayed action or decision
15 Attempting to please everyone all the time
16 Guilt
17 Tiredness
18 Carrying work problems home
19 Dislike of tutorial time, even fear of that period
20 Crossness at being imposed on
21 Headaches
22 I feel I am wasting my time
23 General feeling that the workload is so heavy that it is impossible to cope
24 A tendency to get punch drunk from problems
25 A wish that I could take up another job
26 A tendency to think I must jump to it immediately
27 The feeling of having too many plates spinning on the table at once
28 Irritability
29 Anger which is relieved by dogsbodies e.g. family at home and lower pecking-order colleagues
30 Sleeplessness – especially Sunday night before a new school week
31 Extreme tiredness at times
32 Poor lessons
33 Skin rash

These reactions can be placed in a framework of successive stages which staff pass through as their work (and home) pressures become increasingly severe. In the first stage they develop new coping techniques or continue to use familiar strategies. If these coping actions are unsuccessful in reducing pressures, a number of emotional and mental reactions are experienced. These include frustration, anger, anxiety, fear, poor concentration and memory loss. Severe physical reactions develop when exposure to stress is prolonged. These include heart attacks, ulcers and skin disorders. Continued exposure to the stress situations identified in the previous chapters without a corresponding increase in coping resources brings fatigue, exhaustion and burnout.

This framework is based on three theoretical perspectives which I have found useful in helping teachers understand their reactions to stress. The first theory identifies three stages: the alarm reaction, the stage of resistance and the state of exhaustion. The alarm is invoked when an individual becomes aware of a stress situation. At this stage the hypothalmus stimulates the pituitary gland to secrete the hormone ACTH. This has a knock-on effect, as, when ACTH reaches the adrenal glands, it causes them to release corticoids, adrenalin and noradrenalin. These hormones continue round the body in the bloodstream. They activate the brain, skeletal muscles and the heart, resulting in an increased heart-beat and raised blood pressure.

If the pressures continue and there is little increase in coping strategies the alarm becomes the resistance stage. The increased hormone secretions become regular and the body's resources are weakened (including the immune defence system). The third stage of exhaustion, collapse and burnout may follow with frightening rapidity (Selye 1956).

The second theory examines the relationship between the performance of our tasks at work, the pressures we experience and our stress reactions. This is expressed in figure 9.1. In this theory Hebb (1972) proposed that work with few demands results in poor performance of tasks. Increasing demands are perceived as stimulating and energizing, but if they are beyond the person's coping abilities they lead to high levels of anxiety, poor concentration and reduced effectiveness in one's work. Continued demands, without an increase in coping resources, may lead to fatigue, exhaustion and burnout.

The third theoretical perspective which is helpful in understanding stress reactions also proposes that individuals pass through stress thresholds as they respond to increasing pressures. The first level consists of changes in behaviour which are used by the individual in an attempt to cope with new or increased demands. This is the 'new coping behaviour threshold'. If these attempts are unsuccessful in coping with the situation, the 'frustration threshold' is reached. If there is a continuing failure to cope, individuals may begin to question their competence and will experience strong feelings of anxiety. More severe disturbances may lead to the development of psychosomatic symptoms. As individuals use up their coping resources they will reach and pass through the thresholds of exhaustion and burnout (Appley 1967).

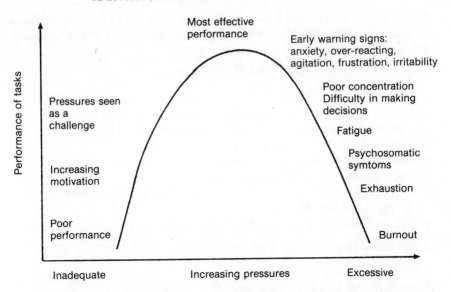

Figure 9.1 The relationship between pressures, work performance and stress reactions

The initial response to pressures which are in excess of coping resources is, according to this theory, to try to use coping actions, for instance discussing the problem with colleagues. In this sense, having to cope with difficulties is beneficial in that it promotes personal and professional development by stimulating the acquisition of additional patterns of behaviour and the strengthening of such personal resources as determination, self-control, tact, adapability, calmness, patience and tolerance. The head of lower school in an inner-city comprehensive school provided a good example of this kind of growth when he wrote: 'this job has made me much more tolerant at work than I would ever have believed possible'.

Teachers' personal characteristics and coping actions – including the three C's of Commitment to a goal, Control over one's work and home circumstances, and perceiving pressures as Challenges rather than threats (Manning *et al.* 1988) – are of considerable significance in tackling stress situations and they are discussed in detail in the next chapter. However the present chapter is concerned with the sequence of reactions when coping strategies are not effective and personal resources are becoming depleted.

Livingstone-Booth (1985) has suggested that this sequence has three stages. Stage one can be recognized 'through the speeding up of all activity; you act rather as if you had an over-active thyroid'.

● You eat faster – often taking a sandwich on the job

- You drink faster – and leave many half-empty cups of coffee or tea to get cold as you do not take the time to really drink one and savour it
- You feel under pressure of time
- You feel as if you are being driven.

Stage two can be recognized by:

- An alteration in your usual sleep pattern (usually waking at 4 or 5 a.m. after taking two or three hours to get off to sleep)
- You over-react to every difficulty
- You become increasingly irritable
- Your memory is not as reliable as it was
- You begin to develop physical symptoms which may include dyspepsia and tension headaches
- You may suffer emotional symptoms such as anxiety and depression.

Stage three can be recognized by:

- Palpitations and chest pain
- Feeling that you may 'pass out'
- Getting any illness that is around
- Difficulty in reaching satisfactory decisions
- Loss of concentration and memory
- All joy, laughter and pleasure have 'dried up'
- Tears seem very near frequently for no reason.

All these stage three reactions in Livingstone-Booth's (1985) model are evidence of exhausted physical, mental and emotional health – which is burnout.

In my workshops teachers report that their first reaction to these situations in school or at home is frequently frustration, which causes a wide range of feelings from irritation to angry aggression. Anger is not necessarily directed at the source of frustration as, for example, when it is the headteacher's inconsistent leadership behaviour which is causing most of the hassles. In these circumstances anger would tend to be displaced to other targets. The next reports indicate that these targets may be the teacher's family. The first is from a male teacher:

> Stress has often caused me to be very hard on my own children and to be irritable at home. Being provoked often by rudeness/abuse, etc. does spill over into private life.

The second report is from a female teacher:

> I usually go home at the end of the day very tense and tired. This sometimes has a bad effect on family life, as it takes quite a few hours to unwind. Often tension is there the next morning.

Armes (1985) in his study of upper school teachers in Bradford, also noted the effects of frustration and irritability on interpersonal relationships:

> The saddest thing is to find that about a third of the teachers with partners or children often have their relationships with them adversely affected.

But the anger caused by frustration is not always expressed overtly either through direct or indirect channels. If it is 'bottled up' for long periods there is a risk of psychosomatic symptoms such as headaches, stomach upsets, sleep disturbances, high blood pressure and skin disorders. A deputy head identified several of these reactions:

> In extreme cases I have headaches, stomach upsets and difficulty in sleeping – all caused, one supposes, by tensions. These never prevent me from attending school.

The relationship between suppressed anger and high blood pressure has been clearly presented by Buss (1961):

> When an individual becomes angry, his blood pressure rises. Since anger is a temporary reaction, the elevation in blood pressure is temporary. Some individuals inhibit the expression of anger and their rage subsides only slowly. They cannot cope with rage, failing to express aggression against those they blame. They remain tense and uncomfortable. As their blood pressure rises more often and stays high for longer periods it becomes a permanent condition.

Suppressed anger has also been reported by the same writer to be crucially involved in the development of some skin disorders. His studies have indicated that unexpressed rage is associated with an increase in the temperature of the skin. These skin changes tend to last longer because the individual is unable to discharge pent-up tension by means of an outburst of aggression. Gradually the reddening of the skin does not disappear and is accompanied by an intense itching.

These different reactions to increasing frustration show several interesting comparisons to the next major emotional response to be discussed. This is anxiety. If feelings of being anxious are slight, teachers may experience a sense of stimulation and alertness which is pleasurable rather than stressful. Increasing demands or more rapid changes or a greater degree of role uncertainty may initiate the arousal of higher levels of anxiety. These may be unproductive in the sense that a teacher's ability to make decisions is impaired or the ability to concentrate is reduced. There may be feelings of panic or an awareness of physiological changes such as accelerated heart rate, more rapid breathing and sweating palms. There may also be a sharp loss o confidence in teaching skills (Cherniss 1980). This reaction was noted by a teacher in a secondary school:

> My major cause of stress is class discipline. When the children don't pay attention I feel very inadequate. I feel I prepare lessons to the very best of my ability and still the lesson doesn't go as I intend it without a fight. A lot of time is wasted making them listen and get on with work. Worrying about this affects my attitude to others at home – I find myself unhappy and consequently irritated by silly little things at home.
>
> I feel that the basic cause of the trouble is my own inadequacy as a teacher, therefore have I any grounds for complaint about my feelings of stress? However, when I talk to others I find they too have problems with class discipline. Are my problems worse than others – or do I just feel they are because it is me?
>
> How do I detach myself from the anxiety? How do I leave the problems at school and not let them interfere with my family life?

When there is prolonged exposure to situations which arouse anxiety or to situations evoking unexpressed frustration and anger physiological changes occur which can lead to the appearance of psychosomatic symptoms. These situations are particularly potent in provoking a high rate of adrenalin secretion. The significance of this physiological change has been clearly stated by a research worker who has been interested for some years in the connection between unfavourable emotional and psychological factors in an organization and the development of stress symptoms. His research results led him to the conclusion that:

> Anxieties, tensions and frustrations as well as sensory annoyances (especially noise) cause the release into the blood stream of adrenalin and other substances which may contribute towards the development of sudden heart attacks.
>
> (Raab 1971:392)

Recent research into occupational stress has tended to confirm these conclusions. The results of the study of 1,790 teachers in England, Scotland, Wales and Northern Ireland conducted by researchers at the Manchester Institute of Science and Technology in 1989 reveal high levels of stress-related illnesses:

> 23 per cent of the teachers reported a 'significant illness' during the previous year including colitis, migraines, heart problems, anxiety attacks, myalgic encephalomyelitis (ME) and irritable bowel syndrome which could have been stress related. Male and

female teachers had significantly higher levels of anxiety and depression than the average population and had levels equal to outpatients in mental hospitals. Male teachers reported significantly more psychosomatic symptoms than average. 13 per cent of the teachers in the sample were taking anti-depressant drugs regularly and 15 per cent were taking them occasionally.

(Travers and Cooper 1990:15)

Travers and Cooper believe that their results suggest that the costs of occupational stress in teaching increased to such an extent in the 1980s that they are now near the top of the occupational league-table for stress. Teachers are, these researchers argue, 'more stressed than most other occupational groups including tax officers, GPs, dentists and nurses'. Moreover their prediction for the 1990s is that teaching and medical practice will move up the league-table from a rating of 'very stressful' to one of 'extremely stressful'.

The implications of these research findings and predictions can perhaps be appreciated more readily by noting some details contained in a report by the Humberside Federation of NAS/UWT (Spring 1991). In their report it is stated that:

secondary school teachers on average lose seven days work a year through stress while in primary schools the figure is 8.5 days a year. Altogether the county's 8,500 teachers take almost 60,000 days off sick every year between them. The county's sixty secondary schools lost in the year 1990-91 an average of 444 days each.

The report noted that the 'LEA has agreed to a suggestion from the NAS/UWT that a working group of teachers and officers should be set up to investigate the problems faced by staff in schools'.

My own research results and those of my students also suggest that teaching has become a more stressful occupation since the first edition of this book was published in 1984. Then I presented information from surveys of staff stress reactions in three comprehensive schools (A,B and C). Now I can compare that analysis with the results from three investigations conducted in 1989 and 1990, two of which (schools Y and Z) were completed by my Bristol University students in their schools (table 9.1).

In school X forty-eight members of staff participated in my INSET workshop. In school Y seventy-five teachers completed my questionnaire and in school Z nine middle-managers participated in the small-scale study. The student in school Y reported:

In my school the majority had experienced irritability (75 per cent), exhaustion (79 per cent) and wanting to leave teaching (62

Table 9.1 Percentage of staff in six English comprehensive schools identifying stress reactions

Stress reactions	% in schools:					
	A	B	C	X	Y	Z
Large increase in consumption of alcohol	0	10	3	21	29	20
Marital or family conflict	3	5	14	44	27	20
The marked reduction of contacts with people outside school	36	22	35	56	54	30
Displaced aggression – on to children or colleagues or people outside school	20	18	14	33	50	30
Apathy	25	18	14	41	50	50
Wanting to leave teaching	25	15	20	56	62	70
Unwillingness to support colleagues	0	0	3	21	10	10
Strong feelings of being unable to cope	7	16	8	28	25	50
Irritability	18	34	24	48	75	70
Moodiness	7	19	22	30	46	40
Inability to make decisions	0	4	6	16	13	20
Feverish activity with little purpose	7	18	10	35	30	20
Inability to concentrate	14	8	10	28	44	50
Absenteeism	0	0	3	8	6	0
Depression	3	11	8	33	58	20
Tension headaches	14	15	18	46	34	30
Feeling of exhaustion	36	46	41	64	79	80
Frustration because there is little sense of achievement	32	30	16	46	75	80
Withdrawal from staff contact	14	7	14	24	14	10
Anger	7	11	12	44	37	30
Anxiety	3	23	16	41	35	40
Loss of sleep	14	15	14	41	30	70
Loss of weight	0	5	0	2	2	0
Feelings of isolation in school	10	8	11	25	27	20
Feelings of fear	0	8	3	21	15	10
Feelings of guilt	7	10	9	25	33	30
Overeating	14	15	14	16	29	10
Skinrash	3	5	0	14	6	0
Large increase in smoking	0	4	9	8	10	0
Hyper-sensitivity to criticism	7	11	18	46	23	10
Back pain	7	8	7	16	21	0

per cent), very often or often in the last academic year. Jack Dunham's checklist in three comprehensive schools nearly ten years earlier shows far lower percentages of those experiencing any of these reactions. It is not possible to draw any definite conclusions from this comparison as the research was not carried out in the same institutions but there is a strong indication that there has been a marked increase in most stress reactions experienced by teachers in the last ten years.

In school Z one of the middle managers was my informant:

I never assumed I was the type of person to be prone to any physical disability due to stress. Of course, I have experienced irritability, tension headaches and exhaustion, but that I took as par for the course. However, three weeks before the end of this summer term I had a wisdom tooth out. This routine operation under local anaesthetic took place, with no complications. I had taken two days off school to recuperate, feeling slightly guilty as I felt reasonably well the following day. That night, however, I caught a very heavy cold and the left side of my lower jaw began to ache. It was not the cavity left by the wisdom tooth that was the problem but the row of teeth in front. The pain did not ease over the weekend. My dentist had gone on holiday and suggested I go to the dental hospital. Here, I was told that the condition I was suffering from was induced by stress, triggered off by the extraction. The pain had resulted from the spasmodic contraction of muscles and a muscle relaxant was prescribed, in fact, a mild sedative. On top of this I caught cystitis – another stress-related condition. It seemed my whole body had given up, just in time for the holidays!

Teachers have always worked under pressure but for many, today's pressures outweigh their ability to cope with them, resulting in stress-related symptoms. As one teacher noted, 'I was very interested to read the stress reactions listed in Jack Dunham's questionnaire. While I have been aware of experiencing many of these feelings, I had no idea that some of them were stress related.'

The reports of two other surveys of stress conducted by my students in their own secondary schools also provide valuable information on the incidence and nature of the stress reactions now being identified by colleagues. The first student's report included the following details:

I distributed a confidential questionnaire to every member of staff – teaching and non-teaching (a total of ninety) – which they had two weeks to complete with the option of discussing their comments further. The response was amazing. Over 50 per cent of the staff returned their questionnaire within a few days. Many commented they had found the venting of their feelings on paper therapeutic and were very willing to talk on a one-to-one basis with me about what they had written. However, one teacher's comments were particularly disheartening:

I began your stress form Friday lunchtime, but I became so agitated and angry about all the frustrations in this god-forsaken business that it was not until 10 p.m. that evening after a few drinks that I finally began to calm down. It's a sign of the depth of my total dismay of this lousy profession that I still can't get the whole stress questionnaire completed.

From the questionnaire it would seem that the signs of occupational stress were evenly distributed between behavioural, emotional, mental and physical — although 25 per cent of the staff who answered said that they suffered from all four categories. One individual included all of the following — under eating, short temper, anger, inability to make decisions, gazing into space, total lack of confidence, nightmares, stomach pains, legs tingling, dizziness. From this it would seem that a large proportion of the staff believe the job is stressful. The management should thus be aware that these signs are having a detrimental effect on the running of the organization as stress is obviously affecting staff's ability to function effectively both in the classroom, at home or as an administrator or manager.

The end of term in particular seemed to be stressful times because staff felt so drained. One member of staff identified a particular day each week:

Sunday night is extremely stressful. I don't want to go to bed 'cos that makes Monday closer. I'm worried about not sleeping, I'm worried that if I have more than two doubles I won't be able to wake up. . . . I often think about ending it all. . . .

The second survey found:

The four main categories of reaction to stress identified by Dunham take the following order of importance: physical, emotional, mental and behavioural. 100 per cent of staff reported feelings of constant tiredness and irritation at times. 50 per cent mentioned headaches, muscular tension including backache, rapid heartbeat, emotional exhaustion and inability to switch off, 33 per cent suffered from feelings of panic at times (and added in one case: 'I think it is probably the coffee!') and 25 per cent were aware of stomach ache, depression and inability to concentrate. One member of staff wrote of reduction in sexual appetite on days when avoidable problems, caused normally by lack of thought from others, presented themselves and another of the accentuation of breathing and asthmatic problems. A member of the office spoke of migraine, visual disturbances and dizziness.

The costs of working in the Education Service in the 1990s in terms of stress-related health problems for some of our teaching and non-teaching colleagues can be recognized from these questionnaire findings. But the costs may become even greater as they reach and pass over the exhaustion and burnout threshold. At the exhaustion threshold feelings of tiredness are different from those usually experienced after a day's work. This is a particular type of tiredness which is often described as 'drained'. A deputy head in a comprehensive school gave a very clear description of this condition and his other symptoms:

> I lose my appetite for life – become withdrawn and morose and totally limp and exhausted. I eat a lot and revert to smoking. My psoriasis gets worse. I am often dizzy and feel muzzy in the mornings – possible blood pressure troubles.

If this level of exhaustion is not relieved by holidays or by absence from school through illness or by taking courses or by having what our American colleagues call 'a mental health day', there is a real risk that the cost will become much greater through burnout. This condition, which one teacher described as 'being a burnt-out husk', has been defined in different ways by research workers and writers but one of the clearest definitions is:

> Burnout is a syndrome of physical and emotional exhaustion, involving the development of a negative self-concept (e.g. poor feelings of personal achievement), negative job attitudes (e.g. discouraged and depressed about work) and a loss of concern and feeling for people.
>
> (Pines and Maslach 1978:3)

It is a severe form of stress reaction which, once it has started, is usually difficult to reverse. The signs of burnout include the physical symptoms of chronic exhaustion, low resistance to illness and alcoholism. Mental symptoms are shown by a deep and pervasive cynicism about work, colleagues, children and the Education System. Behavioural signs are chronic absenteeism and leaving teaching after a period of sickness.

A significant number of these symptoms can be identified in two reports of interviews with a former head of English at a comprehensive school. In her account of her interview with him, Shaw (1986) reported that he left his school at the end of a Thursday afternoon when he was in a dreadful state, utterly exhausted. He went to bed after tea and awoke about 9 o'clock, sweating like a pig and trembling. His wife, also a teacher, said, 'You simply can't go on like this; it's bloody silly' and he made the decision not to return to teaching. He applied for a breakdown pension and eventually three doctors agreed he was unfit to teach. He had been teaching for twenty year and he was 42.

In his interview with me he retrospectively identified the signs of severe stress which at the time he had not recognized as the danger signs of approaching burnout:

- Far, far too many headaches.
- Frequent undue lethargy – I slept or lounged to avoid problems.
- Profuse sweating – increased at times of greatest stress and particularly so in the last few months of my working. This was often diagnosed as some minor viral infection by my doctor and I had days off here and there thinking I'd got some kind of 'flu'.
- Very disturbed sleep patterns.
- A sense of panic and disorientation. This increased very much in the last few weeks.
- An inability to plan work – again this increased suddenly and alarmingly.
- An inability to prioritize (hateful word), i.e. to sort the essential from the trivial.
- Irrational fears and anxieties about aspects of work.
- Profound swings of mood. Depression.
- Failure to cope with projects that I had easily been able to deal with a few years ago.
- Compulsive eating.
- Increasing hostility to change and new ideas at work – a fairly classic indication of failure to cope.

Not all the behavioural, emotional, mental and physical symptoms need to be present to say that a person is burning-out. In any individual some may be present and some not. It is unfortunately still the case that colleagues and members of the senior management team are misreading or ignoring the signals, for example those sent out by two teachers who were former colleagues of one of my students:

> For six months an assistant head of year was exhibiting signs of stress – complaining of not being able to sleep, fatigue and overwork. He had poor feelings of personal achievement, lost his self-esteem, felt useless and became cynical when once he'd been very enthusiastic – but nobody seemed to recognize the symptoms. It was too late when he came into work and collapsed from nervous exhaustion.
>
> A head of department was absent with stress-related illness for two terms. On his return he was put in a position where he was expected to apply for head of faculty role, which he accepted. During the year he was dealing with the pressures of curriculum change but floundering in the classroom, to the point where, in the summer term when GCSE coursework was submitted it was discovered that vast quantities of his classes' work was unmarked.

This caused a crisis and such humiliation for the member of staff that he resigned. By why hadn't this been foreseen? Why had he been encouraged to take on a pressurized role with his recent health record?

These questions forcefully remind us that we should be aware of Blase's (1982) warning that the process of burning-out can be cumulative, as working under long-term pressures leads to the 'gradual erosion' of coping resources. The process may be characterized by a relatively long period of resistance to work stressors followed by a rather rapid increase of symptoms, as in the case of the head of the English department, and finally a total inability to handle any occupational requirements: mental, emotional or behavioural. This happened to another teacher I have helped recently, who found the job more and more of a drudgery, more and more demanding, requiring more and more energy, concentration and willpower to complete hours of marking and preparation in the evenings and at weekends. Finally during a Friday lunchtime he knew he had no more resources left to continue the struggle. He went to his principal to tell him he could not go into his classroom to teach his Friday afternoon classes. Fortunately the principal referred him immediately to his GP, who told him to stay away from college. A year later, after trying to go back to work but not succeeding, and after a short stay in hospital to have in-patient treatment for depression, he applied for and was given an infirmity retirement with an invalidity pension. He was as surprised as his colleagues about the abrupt ending to a successful career of more than twenty years. Neither he nor they had recognized the signs of burning-out.

But a growing number of teachers are apparently aware of severe stress reactions in their collegues, because a number of reports are suggesting that there is an increasing unwillingness to continue in the profession. The study by Travers and Cooper (1990) conducted at the Manchester Institute of Science and Technology was used earlier in this chapter to provide evidence of stress-related illness. It also gives us information about teachers' intentions to leave the profession. About 66 per cent of the teachers in this research project said they had actively considered leaving teaching in the last five years. Almost 28 per cent were looking for alternative employment and 13 per cent were considering early retirement.

A research study was conducted by Smithers and Robinson of the University of Manchester School of Education of 300 secondary teachers in the Christmas term of 1989 (Smithers and Robinson 1990). Half of this group were beginning teaching or taking new posts. The other half were leaving teaching altogether. The teachers who were unwilling to remain had found the costs of stress, particularly being 'overwhelmed by change', much greater than any perceived benefits from remaining ('There must be a better way of earning a living'). So they are leaving for other employment or early retirement, or for family reasons, in increasing numbers, according to Smithers and Robinson, who estimate that the proportion of staff leaving the profession is rising by 1 per cent annually (Smithers and Robinson 1990).

In the light of these conclusions and predictions it is very important to offset this perspective by noting that some teachers have reported that they can handle heavy demands in school without experiencing any major signs of stress. If their coping strategies can be identified and then shared with colleagues a good start will have been made towards stress reduction and prevention. The next chapter is therefore concerned with the resources which teachers use to reduce stress.

10

TEACHERS' COPING RESOURCES

In the last chapter I concluded that exposure to the heavy pressures identified in this book was responsible for the development of a sequence of behavioural, emotional, mental and physical reactions, if the pressures were significantly greater than teachers' coping resources. But my research has also revealed considerable differences between teachers in their responses to similar experiences in school, for example, during reorganization and other major changes some teachers reported few signs of adverse reactions and gave several indications of positive responses such as an increased zest in their teaching. These results directed my attention to the strategies teachers use when they encounter heavy work pressures. I found that they were using a broad range of resources which I shall identify in this chapter as personal, interpersonal, organizational and community.

This view of coping resources is very similar to a number of approaches which have been made towards understanding how people cope with adversities without developing major stress reactions. Caplan (1964) identified the seven characteristics of coping behaviour as:

1 Active search for information
2 Free expression of both positive and negative feelings
3 Asking for help from other people
4 Breaking problems down into manageable bits and working through them one at a time
5 Fatigue countered by pacing of one's efforts
6 Active mastery of feelings where possible but acceptance of lack of control when it occurs
7 Trust in oneself and optimism about outcome.

A study by Mechanic (1967) published three years later proposed that when people attempt to cope with heavy pressures they bring into operation skills, experience, knowledge and personality characteristics in addition to supportive relationships at work, at home and in the community. This perspective suggests that in attempting to understand stress reactions more attention should be given to problem-solving and coping behaviour. The writer argued:

> If we are to understand the stress situation of a man falling out of a boat, the main determinant of how much stress he experiences will be whether or not he can swim.

He argued that the extent to which individuals experience stress in any situation depends on the manner in which they assess both the demands and their competence in dealing with them, and in their preparation of the skills necessary for them to handle these demands with a greater sense of competence.

A third perspective on coping resources which is similar to the one I use in my work with teachers suggests that coping has two functions. First, coping is concerned with changing a situation which is stressful. This may be achieved either by altering the nature of the situation itself or by modifying a person's perception of the situation. The second function of coping is to deal with the thoughts, feelings and bodily reactions to stress rather than to attempt to change the stress situation or a person's perception of it. Both kinds of coping require the use of positive factors which Lazarus calls 'uplifts'. He suggests that the most frequently used are: relating well with a spouse or lover, relating well with friends, completing a task, feeling healthy, getting enough sleep, eating out, meeting responsibilities. visiting, telephoning or writing to someone, spending time with one's family, having pleasurable activities at home (Lazarus 1981).

This list has interesting similiarities with the coping actions identified by teachers in my research and in a study of staff stress in secondary schools in York reported by Kyriacou (1980). In his investigation three different types of resources were identified. The first consisted of talking about problems and feelings to others and seeking support from friends, colleagues and family. The second kind focused on different ways of dealing with the sources of stress. The third type of coping actions was mainly directed towards out-of-school activities and seemed to be aimed at distracting the teachers' attention away from stress at work to more pleasurable and relaxing interests. Kyriacou also asked the teachers which resources they often used to try and reduce stress. The twenty most frequently used coping actions were:

- Try to keep things in perspective
- Try to avoid confrontation
- Try to relax after work

- Try to take some immediate action on the basis of your present understanding of the situation
- Think objectively about the situation and keep your feelings under control
- Stand back and rationalize the situation
- Try to nip potential sources of stress in the bud
- Try to reassure yourself everything is going to work out right
- Do not let the problem go until you have solved it or reconciled it satisfactorily
- Make sure people are aware you are doing your best
- Try to forget work when the school day is finished
- Try to see the humour of the situation
- Consider a range of plans for handling the sources of stress – set priorities
- Make a concerted effort to enjoy yourself with some pleasurable activity after work
- Try not to worry or think about it
- Express your feelings and frustrations to others so that you can think rationally about the problems
- Throw yourself into work and work harder and longer
- Think of good things in the future
- Talk about the situation with someone at work
- Express your irritation to colleagues at work just to be able to let off steam.

A more recent research study using the 'Ways of coping' checklist developed by Lazarus has been presented by Parkes (1988). She investigated the coping strategies that students taking a one-year PGCE course used to deal with a stressful episode. Her findings showed that their stress levels were low when coping strategies were strong and vice versa. Social support was a very significant factor in effective stress management for these student teachers.

My attempts to identify the resources which staff use to reduce stress are based on two methods. I ask them, 'How do you try to reduce your work stress?' and I also invite them to identify their coping strategies on a checklist. Their answers to this question and the items that are ticked on their checklist suggest that they are using a wide range of skills, techniques, knowledge, experience, relationships, thoughts and activities which I have classified as personal, interpersonal, organizational and community resources.

Personal resources include work strategies, positive attitudes and positives pressures such as designing course or lesson material and a certain amount of variety, switching off, trying to come to terms with each stress situation, self-pacing, bringing feelings and opinions into the open, acceptance of the problem and learning the job in more detail. The out-of-school activities which teachers as individuals use to reduce feelings of tension, anger and agitation include gardening, painting, walking, cooking, baking, cycling, driving their cars fast and praying.

The interpersonal resources which teachers use include talking over stressful incidents with their partner, meeting people who are unconnected with teaching and talking to a friend who has a similar job and using him or her as a sounding-board and 'a verbal punching bag'.

Organizational resources come from colleagues in school with whom they are able to discuss their problems, worries and feelings. They also include supportive departmental, pastoral and senior management teams, in-service training and induction courses for probationers and other staff and help from advisers and education officers.

Community activities reported by teachers include bell-ringing, squash, badminton, football, drama and choral singing.

The use of some of these resources in the process of coping with stress is very clearly expressed in the following three reports. The first is from a head of faculty:

How do I cope?
1 Sometimes the very complexity and difficulty of my work makes it enjoyable. I also enjoy leading a team and exercising responsibility.
2 I am a very active person, professionally and socially. I can compartmentalize things.
3 I am a good organizer and within my faculty I have fairly efficient administrative and organizational systems.
4 I keep many projects, at various stages of completion, on the go at once.
5 Usually I can motivate others and lead charismatically.
6 I am fairly lucky in the members of my departmental team who can shift some of the workload away from me.
7 For eight years I practised Martial Arts at a fairly high level, eventually achieving a Black Belt. I occasionally exercise the techniques of restraint and self-control to produce inner and outer calmness that I was taught and picked up in this situation. This is a great help and I tend to remain fairly calm and approachable even under stress.
8 I am still a keen sportsman, playing soccer at weekends and occasionally training and running in the week. This is a great help in relaxing stored-up-aggression.

The second analysis of the coping process was written by a head of sixth form:

My ways of relieving stress factors are varied, but within school the satisfactory completion of a major task in itself helps relieve pressure. Also, for myself, the peaceful interaction in teaching a sixth-form group in my room helps greatly in focusing one's mind and having a chance to enjoy more academic pursuits. At home, I can only fully relax by doing something different, not sitting and thinking about what I haven't done in the day. I need to be active and out enjoying a completely different set of circumstances (mostly away from the people with whom I work).

The third report was written by an MPG teacher:

This coping resource is only employed on days when I am at school. As soon as the bell rings for lunch I leave the school and run four or five miles in the surrounding countryside. I time my return and subsequent exit from the changing room to coincide with the bell for the end of lunch. This activity has now become a vital part of my day. I refuse to give up my lunchtime for any meeting in school and in the early days encountered much hostility from colleagues who felt I obviously had time to spare and that I should be engaged in school work. Explanations about relaxation and the appreciation of the changing seasons, open air and varieties of weather fell on deaf ears. However, I persisted and most staff now accept that I am simply not available for *anything* at lunchtime. This, I feel was the beginning of my discovery of the ultimate coping resource and that is simply that 'it doesn't really matter'. In other words, the root of my beliefs is that school is not my life, but is part of it. It is a job that enables me to feed myself, provide myself with shelter, keep warm and enjoy myself. That is not to say that I am not dedicated. I enjoy my job and take great care over the education of the pupils in my charge, but I have come to realize that, whatever demand is made upon me, it is not so important that it has to dominate my life. I ensure that what needs to be done gets done, but without it controlling or affecting my private life. After the first few times of saying 'no' or apologizing to a class for a delay in marking work, or leaving a meeting early, it is surprising how much pleasanter life becomes, for the simple reason that I am in control of the demands made upon me, rather than the demands controlling me.

The strategy of personal control which is a valuable uplift for this person is one of three essential characteristics (the 'three Cs') of the hardy personality I referred to in the previous chapter who can cope effectively with very stressful situations (Manning *et al.* 1988). The other two traits are commitment, which this teacher's report also identifies, and the perception of work pressures as challenges rather than as threats or as acceptable and enjoyable rather than as sources of stress. My recent research has identified many positive aspects of teachers' work. These include:

- The general 'busyness' of the day and the variety of tasks to get through.
- Interaction with students in a teaching situation.
- Preparation and implementation of new teaching methods or topics not taught before.
- The opportunities to do one's own thing without anyone breathing down my neck.
- The challenge of a constantly changing environment.
- Reading and reflecting and acting on any conclusions.
- The unpredictability of the job – not knowing what might happen during the day.
- Working to deadlines (provided that there aren't too many things working for the same deadlines).
- Trying to find solutions to problems.
- Researching the subject.
- The pressures of preparing, organizing and presenting academic work to students and getting them to the point of peak performance exactly at the time of examinations.
- New challenges when relevant, sensible, etc.
- Lessons which go well.
- Working with others to achieve an outcome.
- Preparing lessons, teaching lessons and marking homework, but even these items are becoming less and less enjoyable because of other pressures.
- All the pressures produced by everyday classroom teaching including conflicts and difficulties are acceptable and produce little or no stress.

The coping methods used by teachers can be seen in the following brief statements, which are grouped into the four categories of personal, interpersonal, organizational and community resources. The personal section is sub-divided into four types: work strategies, positive attitudes, positive pressures and out-of-school activities.

PERSONAL RESOURCES OF TEACHERS
Work strategies

- By working harder – this certainly raises one's self-esteem and not infrequently removes the cause of a stressful situation.
- Making a positive effort to be more efficient and organized.

- By having at least half an hour lunch break daily. I used to work straight through.
- Having in my own mind a clear sense of priorities of what has to be done.
- Spreading the workload by listing essential jobs at the beginning of each week.

Positive attitudes

- Recognizing the dangers of allowing stress factors to combine in my mind so that I reach hyper self-critical conclusions: I'm under stress → I can't cope → I can't teach → I'm an inadequate person.
- Planning several events, including new and interesting activities for future weeks or weekends.
- Say to myself – I have coped before – I will cope now.

Positive pressures

- I enjoy the variety of work.
- Pressure which has a clean finishing point.
- Pressure with a purpose.

Out-of-school activities

- Hard physical exercise. Meditation, relaxation techniques and yoga exercises.
- Cuddling the cats.

INTERPERSONAL RESOURCES OF TEACHERS

The importance of good relationships can be identified in a number of statements concerning the social life of staff, which is as important to them as their school life. The support teachers receive from wife or husband or friends is frequently named as a very positive factor in stress reduction. Three statements can be used to illustrate different aspects of these relationships:

- I reduce stress by talking things through with my husband who isn't in the profession.

- My supportive relationship with my wife is of enormous help, not just in providing overt and tacit reassurance but also because of the physical benefits of a loving and satisfying sexual life.

- I am not afraid of discussing my problems or relating my 'horrific' days with a friend outside school.

ORGANIZATIONAL RESOURCES OF TEACHERS

Information from staff which can be classified under organizational resources is considerably rarer than personal or interpersonal. Support from senior staff is reported, but the importance of good relationships with colleagues is much more frequently described as a positive factor in tackling stress, as the following brief comment illustrates:

Where stress is produced through disagreement with the action of the head I find discussion with colleagues and then the head helps to reduce stress – openness helps!

Another organizational factor is the boost felt after attending a supportive course and the resource potential of this experience can be identified in the following comments. They were written as part of the evaluation by members of my course in staff management at Bristol University. They were responding to the open-ended questionnaire item, 'What were the strongest features of the course?'

- The detailed preparation leading to very searching and relevant questions, the pooling of ideas and original solutions.
- Having a taste of academic life again.
- Stretching one's mind, learning new concepts and writing an academic essay again.
- Meeting other teachers from a variety of schools and backgrounds.
- The opportunity to meet so many friendly and supportive people.
- Learning a great deal which has had a great influence on my own self-perception.
- Enabling me to accept and manage my feelings of stress more easily.
- Your quiet accepting manner, which is just what is needed after a long day at school.
- The confidence you gave me.
- The interesting Thursdays, which I really looked forward to.

COMMUNITY RESOURCES OF TEACHERS

The community activities which teachers report – for example, football, gliding and sailing – seem to have for some of them an importance beyond that of relaxation or pleasure. The activities seem to enable them to assume life-styles which are alternatives to those followed in their professional roles. Their importance was indicated by a head of a mathematics department who wrote:

114

For coping with stress, sometimes I become a workaholic in other directions, since outside school I am a District Councillor and Chairman of a Planning and Development Committee! This involves contact with the public and is an area where I can take decisions and carry the can! I also find walking helps or swimming or playing loud music. I also find, living nineteen miles from school, I have a pleasant journey home through open country which can either help me think through problems or switch off!

The deputy head of a primary school was using a very different lifestyle to reduce his feelings of stress which were mostly caused by his headteacher's non-delegating leadership style:

If things become too irritating I go bell-ringing or don my crash helmet and ride on my extra-curricular motor bike up the M4 at 80 mph. This helps!

These brief reports of personal, interpersonal, organizational and community resources can now be compared with my second method of enquiry, which is the use of a checklist of coping strategies. One of my current checklists was used by one of my students in her school and table 10.1 indicates some of the coping actions of her colleagues.

The stress-reducing techniques of headteachers and deputy heads have also been investigated by asking them the question, 'How do you try to reduce or prevent your work stress?' The resources of deputies include a wide range of work strategies, coping attitudes and organizational support. These methods appear to have replaced to some extent the benefits which their less senior colleagues enjoy from family, friends and community activities. Some examples of these methods follow:

PERSONAL RESOURCES OF DEPUTY HEADS
Work strategies

- Arranging my office (e.g. putting a bolt on the door) so that I can relax undisturbed for a short while before evening functions.
- Coping with the demands means recognizing what they are, learning by experience . . . reading professional literature, visiting other schools, trying to keep an open mind and trying to be objective.
- Arriving at school early (8.00 a.m.) to be available before school begins and to plan my day and try and ensure a clear desk by 8.30 a.m.
- As I get to know the staff, I know the ones whom I can trust and delegate some of the jobs I used to do myself.
- Consider a range of plans for handling sources of stress.

Table 10.1 Percentage of staff in a secondary school identifying coping resources

Coping actions of teachers	%
Working evening and weekends	68
More sporting activities	26
Withdraw from staff to avoid their problems	12
Work harder	30
Deciding priorities and dropping unimportant jobs	54
Catching-up with family life in holidays	56
Dropping low-priority school tasks	26
Closed door strategy	2
Saying to oneself, 'I'll get organized next time'	22
Relaxed breathing	10
Muscle relaxation	10
Exercise	34
Hobby to get away from school mentally	32
Talking to others	54
Working 9 – 5 then forgetting about the job	6
Becoming philosophical – doing what you can but without worrying too much	40
Trying to pretend that a lot of things are not important	8
Planning well ahead	60
Developing different styles of teaching to enable me to cope with a continuous stretch of it	20
Application of Christian faith	18
Compromise	34
Stopping and settling for an unmarked set of books	24
Sod the school work – go out	30
Give up after a point	10
Refusal to do task	4
Backtracking	0
Preparing and marking less well than I would like	60

- List priorities.
- Try to plan my day so that I am available at peak times.
- When stress and pressure is at its peak in school, I leave my office and walk round the school grounds on my own. This gets me away from my desk and gives me the opportunity to clear my head; it generally works very well.
- Coming into school when no staff are present to work out strategies.
- Have a target date for deeper issues.
- Make sure that problems are well defined when you take them to the headmaster.
- Try to be available and to set up routine meetings while the pressure is off.
- Investigate problems as soon as possible.

Positive attitudes

- Accept that many pressures are inevitable and part of the job.

- Think positively – what an interesting and varied job I have!
- Accept that some things will not get done.
- Accept the situation.
- Decide on my own standards for the job rather than those of the head.
- Attempt to discipline myself to doing one thing at a time (not always succeeding).
- Constant self-reminders not to take self and day-to-day crises too seriously.

Out-of-school activities

- A night at home on the headphones and stereo usually works.
- The cat-nap is a technique I use when the work is approaching midnight.
- Keep Saturday totally apart from school whatever!
- Joining an evening class (yoga) to make a complete break from school once a week. Also making determined efforts to attend whatever else is happening however tired I feel.

INTERPERSONAL RESOURCES OF DEPUTY HEADS

- Making strenuous efforts not to work all the weekend but spend at least one complete day with my family.
- By trying to get more involved with my own children.

ORGANIZATIONAL RESOURCES OF DEPUTY HEADS

- I have a very good relationship with colleagues, especially with my immediate most senior colleagues, which facilitates and makes more effective our mutual support.
- By teamwork and reliance on other colleagues.
- Finding allies among the staff to try to disseminate my ideas.
- Have a good personal relationship with staff.
- Teaching is my haven.
- Have a few colleagues with whom (in different areas of work) it is possible to let off steam and explode in frustration.
- Talk in relaxed way to people even if (especially when!) uptight.
- I unload on the head and the other deputy.

COMMUNITY RESOURCES OF DEPUTY HEADS

- Find activities entirely different from school.
- Going away every holiday period and half-term.

- Every weekend to have a 'treat' built in – the greater the stress in the week, the greater the 'treat'.

The strategies of headteachers are similar to those identified by their deputies though heads appear to have a wider range of relationships available to them at the organizational level and they seem to be able to make greater use of community activities. The following reports illustrate their attempts to reduce stress:

PERSONAL RESOURCES OF HEADTEACHERS
Work strategies

My decision to be firm about boundaries has been particularly helpful to me in coping with stress. I made the decision never to take work home and to have a set limit to evening and holiday work at school. While this is sometimes more honoured in the letter than the spirit – i.e. I do take inner worries if not paperwork home – I think it has helped.

Positive attitudes

The importance of identifying the sources of stress has been clearly articulated by the head of a primary school:

In looking back and trying to decide what was particularly stressful in the past two years I find it quite difficult first of all to distinguish what was usually stressful and what was a normal strain of the work.

I think that stress can be distinguished through its effect of lack of sleep, anxious waking or waking very early and feelings of depression about work. On the other hand it is not quite that easy because I might be awake thinking about an important decision without feeling any undue sense of strain or depression (maybe excitement) and at other times feelings of stress may seem to be due to an accumulation of minor things (especially at the end of term) – in fact the stress is perhaps worst where there is nothing to which it can be directly attributed – and it may be that once a source of stress is identified it immediately becomes less stressful.

Out-of-school activities

I practise meditation regularly, which produces effortless relaxation (morning and evening). The morning session makes me alert and ready for the day and is a preventive measure against stress building up during the day due to the inner relaxation it produces.

In the evening after a hard day's work I am able to totally relax (twenty minutes) which neutralizes any accumulated tension, either muscular or mental that may be present.

INTERPERSONAL RESOURCES OF HEADTEACHERS

I have become aware of the need for support and supervision, of the value of someone outside the situation who can help one to see things which are blocked or difficult in a relationship and where I am reacting unconsciously or defensively. I have found some such support through encounter groups, personal relationship courses and more recently through training as a marriage guidance counsellor. I think this has helped me to come to terms with my own stress and worry and to be more able to help others cope with theirs.

ORGANIZATIONAL RESOURCES OF HEADTEACHERS

Staff support

I feel my stress is greatly reduced by the good relationship between the staff and me. We discuss all problems extensively and very informally and although obviously the responsibility rests with me, the support of the staff in invaluable to me.

The deputy head

The deputy head has a special role as someone whom I see regularly and with whom I can talk openly, trying out alternatives, thinking through possibilities, sharing my doubts or fears and arriving at a decision that I feel is broader-based than if I tried to sort it out on my own.

Senior management team

My stress has been considerably reduced by the opportunity to discuss with the senior management team the problems in school. I find that unloading my stress upon them relieves me of my own stress.

The governors

There has been considerable support and active interest in the school by the governors. Also we are again fortunate in that there are no personality clashes.

Outside professional support

Other heads and the Advisory Service have provided valuable support in that they are prepared to take the time to listen while I talk out a problem with them. This is sometimes all it takes to solve the particular problem.

The pupils

The children have been a surprisingly supportive resource. I made an educational point of involving and informing them (the over-eights) with the developments of the school-closure crisis and the resulting comments, work and supportive feelings that have come back have been very encouraging.

COMMUNITY RESOURCES OF HEADTEACHERS

I reduce stress by ensuring that my life is not on a single track. I do this by pursuing other interests – mainly music and sport – so that on Monday mornings my body and spirit are refreshed.

I find that as a member of a motor racing club being at a race meeting blocks out all other thoughts.

As a Chief Observer in the Royal Observer Corps I have different responsibilities towards my crew and this helps to focus attention away from school.

Two heads sent me their clearly defined frameworks of the factors which sustain them as they tackle the pressures of being the head of a primary school and the head of a comprehensive school. I would like to use them as concluding summaries to this chapter. In the framework of the primary school head there are ten strategies:

1 Make full use of rubbish bin
2 Sort out the trivial from the important
3 Talk through any anxieties with another person
4 Sleep on a problem
5 Go and work with the children
6 Do not allow my working life to intrude into my private life
7 Have a large gin and tonic on Friday evenings
8 Take the dog for a long walk
9 Try to keep lines of communication as open as possible
10 Remember to laugh.

In the framework of the head of the comprehensive school there are five major areas:

1 *Family Life* I am happy and secure with an understanding wife.
2 *Job Satisfaction*
    (a) good pay and a high standard of living
    (b) challenge of the job
    (c) I enjoy being a headteacher
3 Access to *supportive colleagues* at the same level of management and also I have the school management team to whom I can delegate responsibility.
4 *Leisure activities*: squash, cricket, music, mountaineering and special short term interests such as rewiring the house and photography.
5 *Switching off from work*
    (a) by living away from the school community
    (b) by mixing with people whose interests are not educational
    (c) by having the pleasure of two children

This list can also be used to provide a link between this chapter and the next. This head's self-analysis identified a rich store of renewable resources. If the reports from other heads and teachers are reliable sources of information, his coping potential is stronger than many of his colleagues who cannot find satisfying activities in their communities, nor do they have the support of caring teams in school. They may not be able to talk freely with their colleagues because they do not trust them and they may possess only a few of the resources identified in this chapter. It is therefore realistic to suggest that many teachers need to learn to use more coping strategies. A wide range of personal, interpersonal, organizational and community attitudes, actions and activities has been discussed in this chapter and this list provides a sound basis for anyone wanting to learn to deal with work pressures more effectively. But it is possible to add to this store and the next two chapters discuss further recommendations for reducing stress. The first is concerned with methods of strengthening personal and interpersonal resources.

11

RECOMMENDATIONS FOR STRENGTHENING PERSONAL AND INTERPERSONAL RESOURCES

The coping strategies which you and your colleagues use in school and when you are away from work provide a valuable bank of resources from which each of you can make withdrawals to meet the demands you face. But it is important to know that the deposits in the bank can be increased by learning and practising new skills. This will help you to prevent the onset of harmful effects of stress such as illness and enable you to manage the changes in your role in the post-Reform Act era with confidence, competence and effectiveness. Preparation and prevention can be achieved by planning and putting into practice as soon as possible a stress-management programme, either alone or preferably with your colleagues. This programme could be based on your own ideas of what could be helpful. It could also include one or more of the following recommendations for strengthening coping strategies.

Much has been written about how to cope more effectively with stress. Panaceas have been authoritatively recommended – relaxation, diet, exercise, meditation and bio-feedback have each been proposed as the definitive method. Lists of stress-reducing actions have also been published. It has been suggested by Kyriacou (1980) that there is a considerable similarity between these lists in that five maxims form the core of the advice given. These are:

- get things in perspective
- analyse yourself and your situation
- recognize your limitations
- pamper yourself
- relax.

One major problem with these packages of advice is that no attempt is made to help people relate their needs to the recommendations. Another difficulty is that there is no suggested framework which can be used for the integration of recommendations into a coherent, individualized

122

stress-reduction programme. In my work with teachers in conferences, courses, counselling and now in this book I use the following framework:

GROUNDRULES FOR LEARNING HOW TO REDUCE STRESS

1 Accept the possibility of the existence of stress in your colleagues and yourself.
2 Learn to understand what stress is.
3 Begin to tackle the problem by identifying the pressures from change, role conflict, poor working conditions and pupil behaviour in your school.
4 Learn to recognize your reactions to pressures, for example, in your behaviour and relationships, emotions, thinking and the reactions in your body.
5 Identify your coping strategies at work and outside work.
6 Develop stress-reduction training programmes at the individual/ department/pastoral-team/whole-school levels which will enable you to develop a wide range of personal, interpersonal, organizational and community resources which you can use to deal with your pressures and reactions.

ACCEPTANCE OF STRESS

This first step in the six-point programme is very difficult for some colleagues because of the stigma which is unfortunately still firmly associated with stress in their minds. The effects of this negative factor on starting stress-management programmes can be readily appreciated in the following report from an experienced teacher on my Bristol University Professional Studies course:

> At my previous school the male-dominated hierarchy was very much one which would not admit to the stress of the job and the typical response to stress caused by disruptive pupils was a dismissive 'I don't have any trouble with them'. This had a particularly detrimental effect on male staff, who felt they would be regarded as weak if they let stress show, and most of the women staff would not admit to stress either because these men were rather chauvinistic.

Another teacher emphasized the importance of this first step because of her personal experience of stress:

> I've learnt not to be too proud to ask for help! I now know that

acknowledging anxiety to yourself and expressing it to the right people is the first step in relieving it. Having had a complete breakdown I would plead with anyone to acknowledge stress long before it gets to that stage.

So in your school it may be necessary to fight the stigma. You have the right to express your feelings openly without fear of cynical comments from colleagues about being weak or inadequate or incompetent or female! My experience suggests that when one or two people begin to open up about their feelings – perhaps anxiety about the new forms of assessment – other members of staff who have been waiting for a lead soon begin to follow and to start to feel the benefit of not inhibiting their feelings.

It may also be necessary to challenge some beliefs about teaching which may have been held very strongly by you and your colleagues for a number of years. This process of learning may be slow and painful, but it is essential for the rest of the programme. Now will you please consider the following beliefs. If you have them they will probably hinder your attempts to reduce stress, so some rethinking will be necessary. The beliefs are:

1 My job is my life and my life is my job.
2 In my position I must be totally competent, knowledgeable and able to help all the staff (or children). I must always work at my peak level with a lot of energy and enthusiasm.
3 To be able to accomplish my job and for my self-esteem I must be liked and respected by everyone I work with.
4 Getting any form of negative feedback about my work indicates that there is something wrong in what I am doing.
5 Things must work out the way I want them to.

These beliefs can be held so strongly that they become self-induced pressures. They represent unrealistic expectations about one's capabilities, especially perhaps in relation to time pressures. You can assess some of the demands you are making on your own resources by completing the following questionnaire:

1 Do you feel there are not enough hours in the day to do all the things you must do?
2 Do you always move, walk and eat rapidly?
3 Do you feel an impatience with the rate at which most events take place?
4 Do you say 'Uh-huh, uh-huh', or 'yes, yes, yes, yes' to someone who is talking, unconsciously urging them to 'get on with it' or hasten their rate of speaking? Do you have a tendency to finish the sentences of others for them?

5 Do you become unduly irritated or even enraged when a car ahead of you in your lane runs at a pace you consider too slow? Do you find it anguishing to wait in a line or to wait your turn to be seated in a restaurant?
6 Do you find it intolerable to watch others perform tasks you know you can do faster?
7 Do you almost always feel vaguely guilty when you relax and do absolutely nothing for several hours?
8 Do you attempt to schedule more and more in less and less time and in doing so make fewer and fewer allowances for unforeseen contingencies?

These questions need to be considered very carefully by all teachers, but especially those who are 'neglecting all aspects of their life except work, who are ambitious, impatient and involved in a chronic incessant struggle to achieve more in less and less time' (Friedman and Rosenman 1974). The modification of their attitudes to work and time are so important because research studies have concluded that these so-called 'Type A' men and women, who answer yes to the above questions, are 'coronary-prone', that is they have an increased risk for all forms of cardiovascular disorders leading to heart attacks. This is compared with 'Type B' individuals, whose life-styles are the opposite of the overdriven type A patterns. These findings have been challenged, but a recent authoritative review concludes that type A is an important risk factor for CHD (Coronary Heart Disease) especially if it is associated with high levels of anger and hostility (Johnston 1989).

Meichenbaum (1983) has proposed that one should begin to change a type A style of living by following five suggestions:

1 Spend time alone in meditation or in deep relaxation.
2 Do things singly and avoid trying to do two or more things simultaneously
3 Allow yourself plenty of time, whether it be working, eating, talking, listening or playing.
4 Learn to spend time enjoying things such as music, reading, exercise and hobbies.
5 Allow these enjoyable experiences to enhance your life as a whole, providing stimulation, exercise or relaxation rather than considering them to be a waste of time or as a chance to exhibit your superiority.

These suggestions will help workaholic teachers to gain a greater control over their time management at work. The successful utilization of available work time also means there is less stealing of non-work time which is needed for family, recreation and creative activities. This ensures that there will be time and energy for out-of-work interests, hobbies and activities which balance and are complementary to work experiences. There will also be more time and energy for thinking, planning and preparation for the successful management of the changes which are affecting teachers at an increasing rate.

So that you can achieve more effective management of your work time you may like to have the following recommendations from an experienced head of department:

1 Be prepared to write down tasks as they are received.
2 Construct a weekly list based on order of importance.
3 Allot tasks to approriate time slots during the week.
4 Undertake more thought-orientated tasks at times when freshest. If necessary divide up lengthy tasks into small units.
5 Look for tasks that can be discarded.
6 Identify sources which will enable rapid and successful completion of tasks.
7 Try to avoid taking on more than is reasonably possible to complete.
8 Check off tasks once completed.
9 Try to ensure that some time is left available for emergencies or nothing in particular.

THE MEANING OF STRESS

When you have started to accept that stress may be causing problems for you and you are beginning to change your attitudes to work, particularly if you are experiencing self-induced pressures, you may like to pay attention to the second groundrule for stress management programmes and training. This is to work out the meaning of stress for yourself. It does not mean, in my view, that if you say you are suffering from stress you are incompetent, weak or a failure. What does it mean then? This is an important question because staff have different definitions of stress and their perspective determines what they mean when they say they are or are not under stress. One definition sees stress as external pressures, for example, the stress of reorganization or poor working conditions. A second definition describes stress as the reactions to these pressures, for example, emotional reactions like anger and physical reactions such as tension headaches. A third definition includes both pressures and reactions and also includes the coping resources which teachers use as they attempt to reduce their pressures and reactions. Stress from this perspective means a significant excess of pressures over coping resources, which leads to the development of positive and negative reactions. This is the definition used in my workshops.

IDENTIFYING PRESSURES AND STRESS REACTIONS

The third and fourth groundrules are the identification of the work pressures on you and your colleagues and the stress reactions you and they are experiencing which indicate that these pressures are not being managed effectively. Many people refuse to recognize these symptons and attempt to externalize everything by concentrating blame for situations that are stressful on to other people's inadequacies, ignorance or incompetence. It may be possible to review these signs of stress (excess of pressures over coping strategies) by talking things over with a friend or in your team at school.

IDENTIFYING COPING STRATEGIES

The fifth groundrule must be therefore to identify your coping strategies at work and outside work. Special notice should be taken of any resources or activities you have dropped recently because of pressure of work or, ironically, because of increased stress. You may for instance have stopped playing squash or swimming or going out with friends because you feel you 'can't be bothered' or are too tired in the evening.

You may find the idea of using your resources to reduce stress a new one. It certainly was for one of my course members this year:

I had never thought about my personal coping strategies until I started to discuss this as part of the course. Strategies like dressing differently outside school, keeping home life as separate as possible, not going out with teachers on a regular basis and getting away at weekends were not anything I associated with stress management until recently, but this course has taught me that you need to be able to identify those strategies you have and those which need introducing, strengthening or altering to improve your ability to cope with stress.

DEVELOPING STRESS-REDUCTION PROGRAMMES

The sixth and final groundrule is to make recommendations for strengthening your resources by means of stress-management strategies for yourself and, with your colleagues, stress-management policies for the whole school staff. These recommendations can be made from the reports and suggestions from teachers I discuss in this chapter and in the final chapter, or from INSET days which you and your colleagues might arrange. They could include specific policies and strategies to tackle the pressures you have identified.

This training phase also includes learning and practising new skills and one of the most important will possibly be relaxation. Few of the teachers I work with have taken a course in relaxation training. There are several different methods available, some starting at the feet and working upwards and some working from the scalp downwards. There is no best method. Teachers who are particularly tense in the muscles of their legs and abdomen like to work upwards and those with painful neck and shoulder muscles like to progress from the head. Three methods are given in some detail so you can practise them and decide which is appropriate for you. The first one starts at the feet:

Relaxation skills as personal resources

Relaxation training will help you cope with stress situations and stress reactions. Once you have mastered the necessary skills you can use the relaxation response to cope with stress as soon as you begin to perceive it. Practise the first relaxation exercises at least twice a day until you master them. At first they will need a practice session of half an hour, but soon you will master the skills in a shorter time. Each part of the body is tensed and relaxed in turn from the feet upwards. The procedure for the upper part of the body may be used to illustrate the techniques. Press the palms of your hands together and push your finger tips hard to tense your chest and shoulder muscles. Hold the tension for 5 seconds and let it out halfway for an additional 5 seconds. Now relax those muscles completely.

Controlled breathing is one of the most important elements of the relaxation programme because you can relax by breathing properly. When your chest is filled, hold your breath for about 5 seconds, then exhale slowly for about 10 seconds.

Relaxation training exercises

The second approach formulated by Murgatroyd and Woolfe (1982) starts at the head. To practise the routine it is best to lie on the floor or to sit in a position which helps you to feel comfortable. Regular practice of this brief routine each day will also aid in the reduction of stress and increase the ability to cope with stressful situations.

1 Lie down on your back or sit in a chair which supports your back.
2 Close your eyes and try to block out any sounds. Think only of these instructions.
3 Think about your head. Feel the muscles in your forehead relaxing. Let any creases just drop away. Relax your eyelids. Relax your jaw. Let your tongue fall to the bottom of your mouth. Begin to breath deeply.

128

4 Relax your shoulders – let your arms go loose.

5 Relax your neck – let your head roll until you find a comfortable position.

6 Think about your left arm. Tense it then relax it. Tense it again and relax it slowly. Concentrate on it from the shoulder to the tip of your fingers. Let any tension in the arm flow from your fingers. Let this arm become relaxed.

7 Do the same for your right arm.

8 Think about your left leg from the hip to the knee and from the knee to the tip of your toes. Tense your left leg and then relax it. Tense it harder and then relax it as slowly as you can. Let any tension in this leg flow from your toes. Let this leg become relaxed.

9 Do the same for your right leg.

10 Listen now to any sound from within your body – your breathing, your heartbeat, your stomach. Pick one of these sounds and focus on it. Exclude other thoughts from your mind.

11 After about 2–3 minutes slowly open your eyes, sit upright and stretch your arms and legs fully.

Deep relaxation

The third type of relaxation training also starts at the head. Deep muscular relaxation is a skill so it requires training and practice. When the skill has been achieved you will have an ability to notice relatively small changes in muscular tension and you may become aware for the first time how frequently you have been tense without realizing it. Your training and practice will enable you to turn off even intense emotional responses quite rapidly. This approach uses a script which I have recorded and played on many teachers' courses and conferences. I am giving you the script so you can prepare your own tape:

> This recording will help you learn the skill of deep relaxation which is so important for stress reduction, stress management and overall health and well-being . . . sit comfortably, in a relaxed position and concentrate your mind fully on these instructions . . . take a deep breath, and as you let it out, allow your eyes to fall shut . . . let your body begin to relax and unwind . . . take another deep breath, and as you exhale let it carry all the tension out of your body . . . allow a feeling of peacefulness to descend over you . . . a pleasant, enjoyable sensation of being comfortable and at ease . . . now turn your attention to your body and begin to pay close attention to the sensations and signals you can detect . . . find the place or the muscle that is most strongly tensed or exerted and allow it to let go of its hold . . . begin to let all your

muscles, all over your body, give up their hold and begin to go limp . . . now direct your attention to the top of your head and allow a feeling of relaxation to begin there . . . allow it to spread downward through your body . . . let the small muscles of your scalp relax . . . let the muscles of your forehead relax . . . devote special attention to your forehead and feel the muscle there giving up its hold . . . feel your eyebrows sagging down and let your eyelids become very heavy . . . let all the muscles around the back and on the sides of your head relax completely . . . imagine that your ears are even drooping under their own weight . . . and now let your jaw muscles relax and allow your jaw to drop slightly . . . don't deliberately open or close your jaw, just let it float freely . . . allow the muscles of your cheeks and lips to relax and grow limp . . . now, all the muscles of your face and head have given up their hold and are very relaxed . . . now, let the muscles of your neck relax slightly, keeping them exerted only enough to hold your head upright and balanced easily in position . . . let your shoulders become heavy and sag downwards as you relax the muscles that come down from the sides of your neck to the shoulders . . . let the feeling of relaxation continue to spread downward to the muscles of your chest and upper back . . . command those muscles to release their hold . . . you have no need of them for the time being . . . let your shoulder muscles go completely limp and let your arms rest heavily with your hands in your lap or on your thighs . . . feel your arms growing very heavy . . . relax all the muscles of your forearms, hands and fingers . . . you have no desire whatever to move any single muscle in your entire body . . . pay attention to your breathing for a few seconds and notice how it has become regular and shallow . . . now let the feeling of deep relaxation spread fully down into your chest, down through the muscles of your back and down into your arms . . . allow your stomach muscles to relax completely . . . your stomach will probably sag just a bit as the muscles release their hold . . . relax the muscles of your sides, shoulder blades and the small of your back . . . let the muscles of your spine relax – the ones on either side of your spine that run from the base of your skull down to the tip of your spine . . . keep them exerted only enough to keep your back in position . . . now relax the large muscles in your thighs . . . let them go completely limp . . . feel all your muscles so relaxed that they begin to feel as though they are turning to jelly . . . your entire body is becoming profoundly relaxed . . . relax the muscles of your buttocks and the muscles underneath your thighs . . . let the muscles of your calves relax . . . be sure to relax the muscles on the front of your lower legs and shin muscles . . . let your

ankles feel free and loose . . . now wiggle your toes once or twice
and let all the little muscles of your feet give up their hold
completely . . . now your whole body is extremely relaxed, and
we're going to concentrate on certain areas in order to increase
this feeling of profound relaxation even more . . . pay close
attention to the sensations in your arms . . . by now, your hands
and feet will have become somewhat warm, due to the increased
circulation of blood in them . . . tune into this feeling of slight
warmth and allow it to increase . . . don't try to make it happen
. . . allow your arms to feel extremely heavy and completely limp
. . . feel this growing sensation of warmth spreading out to your
fingertips . . . concentrate closely on your hands and arms . . .
allow the feeling of pleasant heaviness and warmth to increase by
itself . . . simply observe the process and encourage it . . . now, let
those same feelings of heaviness and warmth spread through
your legs . . . concentrate closely on the sensations in your legs
and let them become very, very heavy . . . very heavy and very
warm . . . arms and legs becoming so heavy and so warm . . . your
entire body is profoundly relaxed and you feel only a pleasant
overall sensation of heaviness, warmth, and absolute peace . . .
now turn your attention to your breathing and without interfer-
ing with your breathing in any way, simply begin to observe it . . .
feel the slow, peaceful rise and fall of your stomach as the breath
moves slowly in and slowly out of your body . . . don't try to hurry
it up or slow it down . . . just act as a casual observer, taking a
curious interest in this slow, steady process . . . imagine you have
just discovered this steady rising and falling of your stomach and
you are observing it with curiosity and respect . . . wait patiently
for each breath to arrive and notice its passing . . . notice the brief
periods of quiet after one breath passes and before the next one
arrives . . . now continue to observe this breathing process and
begin to count your breaths as they arrive . . . as the first one
comes watch it closely and hear yourself say 'one' . . . wait
patiently for the next one and count 'two' . . . continue until you
have counted fifteen breaths, not allowing any other thoughts to
distract you . . . now you are deeply relaxed and you can return to
this peaceful state whenever you want to . . . take a few moments
to pay close attention to this relaxed feeling all over your body and
memorize it as carefully as you can . . . store the entire feeling of
your whole body in your memory, so that later you can retrieve it
and relax yourself at will . . . now, before you return to full
altertness and activity, take plenty of time to wake up your body
and bring it back to its usual level . . . wiggle your fingers and toes
. . . shrug your shoulders, move your arms and legs a little bit

. . . keeping your eyes closed for a few moments longer, make sure you can sense all parts of your body . . . use your hands to massage your thigh muscles and the muscles in your arms . . . move your head around a little bit, . . . now, take a nice deep breath and allow your body to feel fully alive and flowing with plenty of energy . . . and now open your eyes.

This recording, which uses a script adapted from one prepared for industrial management training by Albrecht (1979) takes about twenty minutes to play. It has been used by many teachers after they have participated in my workshops. Not all teachers find it useful but it has been of benefit as the following comments suggest, though the importance of practice should be noted:

Thank you for sending me your tape. I have so far found it very effective at the time of listening, in as much as I fall momentarily into sleep and that is certain to be a great benefit. I have once or twice tried to recall it to mind when I have been unable to sleep during the night and I expect that when I have practised a little more I shall have the added benefit of unbroken nights.

I have played your tape through once and felt quite good. However I do think that a great deal of practice is needed. On my return to school on Thursday morning I was immediately inundated with problems which had built up over the two previous days but was able to tackle them much more calmly. They don't go away, they never do, but I did not end up with the usual splitting headache. All this makes it sound as though my life is continual tensions – it is not, but there are times when it does get too much. I am not pretending to be an expert in so short a time but I do feel stronger.

These three programmes are just a small sample of methods which are available to achieve relaxation. Yoga exercise and meditation are other possibilities available to teachers.

Meditation

The use of meditation was strongly recommended by the headteacher of a primary school and many teachers will be interested in his comments:

As a founder member of the British Meditation Society I am very interested in informing headteachers about the use of meditation as an antidote to, and as a preventitive measure against stress. I have taught many practising teachers, including one headmaster, to relax in this way and all find real benefit. Regular introductory talks and courses of instruction in the theory and practice of meditation are available in most parts of the country. The more I meditate the easier it becomes to cope with stress – I find myself staying calm and controlled in situations where it would be very easy to flare up or become emotionally involved. Many research projects have shown the depth of relaxation obtained through meditation and doctors are increasingly recommending patients to take up meditation.

These meditative disciplines aim to help the practitioner to reach a special level of mind by clearing from it all conscious thoughts. This produces a pleasant calm and goes a long way towards relieving and preventing illness caused by tension. This level of mind is called by some practitioners 'going into Alpha': 'when you are daydreaming or just going to sleep but not quite there yet or just awakening but not yet awake, you are in Alpha' (Silva and Mieli 1977). This level of brain activity is 'inner consciousness'. It can be compared to a higher level of brain activity when we are fully awake which is called Beta or 'outer consciousness'. A much earlier and clearer description of an Alpha mind-level came from Wordsworth, who wrote the lovely phrase, 'A happy stillness of mind'.

To reach this blissful state it is necessary to learn to meditate in a certain way. According to Silva, who developed a special 'Mind-Control' technique and has used it with many hundreds of thousands of people in the United States and several other countries, this is what should be done:

> Lie down or sit in a comfortable chair with your feet on the ground. Close your eyes and look upward, behind your eyelids at a 20 degree angle. Now slowly, about two-second intervals, count backwards from one hundred to one. Use the hundred to one method for ten practices. Then count only from fifty to one in another ten practices – then from twenty-five to one, then ten to one and finally five to one – each time for ten practices. To come out of Alpha use the same method each time – say to yourself – I will slowly come out as I count from one to five, feeling wide awake and better than before. One – two, prepare to open your eyes – three – four – five eyes open, wide awake feeling better than before.
>
> (Silva and Mieli 1977:17).

Silva suggests that this backward counting method may not always bring inner peace, calm and deep relaxation for people experiencing severe pressures. It many be necessary to use additional skills. He recommends:

Sit in a comfortable chair with your feet flat on the floor or lie down. Now concentrate on first one part of the body, then another to consciously relax it. Start with your left foot and finish with your scalp. Now pick a spot about 45 degrees above eye level on the ceiling or the wall opposite you. Gaze at this spot until your eyelids begin to feel a little heavy and let them close. Start your countdown from fifty to one. Do this for ten practices, then ten to one for another ten practices, then five to one. Establish a routine of meditating two or three times a day about fifteen minutes a session.

(Silva and Mieli 1977:29).

At the end of each backward-counting sequence Silva recommends the practice of visualization. We should imagine a large screen about 6 feet in front of our eyes. On to the screen we project whatever we want to concentrate on – in three dimensions and in full colour – perhaps our ideal place of relaxation. Silva also argues that visualization can be used more positively for 'dynamic meditation' to improve memory, to speed learning and to improve health. He believes that 'we already know enough to strengthen with our minds the body's repair forces so that illness can be combatted more successfully (Silva and Mieli 1977:29).

Exercise

These stress-reduction programmes which are based on meditating and relaxation skills will help you to 'unhook' yourself from the responsibilities and worries of work, but they might be too passive for some colleagues whose feelings of tension, frustration and anger need more active ways of expression outside work. These activities could be directed towards the important aim of becoming and keeping physically fit. They could include any exercise which makes you breathe heavily but does not cause you to get out of breath. This means that the activities – jogging, cycling, fast walking, swimming, etc – can be continued for long enough to bring pleasure and satisfaction without discomfort. There should be at least one of these activities each day and you might find you enjoy beginning each day with:

Jack's six-minute loosener

1 Circular arm swinging. Start with your arms by your sides. Swing backwards and over your head, stretching your arms a little as you do this. Bring your arms down to the starting position. Repeat twenty times.
2 Repeat by going up on tiptoes as your arms are stretched over your head. Repeat twenty times.

3 Arms by your sides. Allow your trunk to fall to the left until your fingers touch the side of your knee. Resume upright position. Repeat ten times. Now use the same exercise to your right side; repeat ten times.

4 Arms by your sides. Turn your body to the left, keeping your feet still, until you are looking immediately behind you. Return to the front position. Repeat ten times. Now use the same exercise, turning to the right, and, repeat ten times. Now use the same exercise, turning to the right, and, repeat ten times.

5 Bend your knees, keeping them close together with your back straight, and arms extended forwards. Go down as far as you can. Come up to standing position. Repeat twenty times.

6 Gentle running in the same space until you have counted 200.

If you think that exercises are only for physical fitness fanatics you may be reluctant to accept them as important ways of reducing stress, so, when you start, start slowly and build up gradually. You will find after a few weeks that you are giving these exercises the same priority as other routine activities such as cleaning the car or housework or shopping. When you begin to feel the positive effects of your health and fitness programme in terms of increased stamina, suppleness and strength you should consider further improvements. The recommendations of the Health Education Authority are helpful:

> If no one specific activity appeals to you, that doesn't mean that there is no way you can achieve reasonable fitness. Try walking at every available opportunity. Leave the car at home when you go to the shops. If you take the bus to work get off a couple of stops early. If you work in an office block leave the lift and take to the staircase. Climbing stairs is a very good stamina-building activity.

Exercise is a potent factor in reducing stress in a number of ways:

1 It strengthens the body's defences against infection by releasing protein from the muscles and preventing the build-up of various steroids including cortisone.

2 It improves respiration by relaxing the diaphragm and activating the lungs, which increases the amount of oxygen in the blood.

3 It releases stored up aggression.

4 It restores physical and mental equilibrium.

5 It reduces the risk of stress-associated hypertension.

I can illustrate the advantages of exercise by quoting from my interviews with teachers:

> I use hard physical exercise to reduce stress.

I am still a keen sportsman, playing golf at weekends and occasionally training in the week. This is a great help in releasing stored up aggression.

I ride a bike to school. It takes me an hour each way, which gives me plenty of time to think out strategies to face the day. At the end of the day I leave as soon as possible rather than re-hash what has happened because I am totally drained. By the time I arrive home I have usually got back to a balanced state of physical and mental equilibrium.

The link between health and exercise and the ability to cope effectively with stress has been studied by Professor Steptoe and his colleagues at the Department of Psychology of St George's Hospital Medical School. They have shown that normal adults benefit psychologically from regular physical activity. Experiments were set up with volunteers who did 20 minutes of vigorous rhythmic exercise three or four times a week. These volunteers were compared with others who carried out light, non-vigorous exercise over the same time. Anxiety, tension and depression levels were measured before and after the programme. Ten weeks of the moderate exercise schedule were enough to reduce tension and anxiety, clear up mental confusion and improve ability to cope with stress in the vigorous exercisers. The effects were much greater than those recorded in the light exercisers and were found in people with normal stress levels and in those suffering from high levels of stress and tension. (The Health Promotion Research Trust 1989).

Out-of-school activities

This analysis of a coping strategy is important for another reason. It provides a persuasive argument for out-of-school activities which balance and are complementary to school actions and experiences and which provide alternative rhythms to the pace of school life. These interests and hobbies have a much wider range than physical fitness exercises. They include those which are manual skills such as gardening, woodwork, and house-painting, musical activities, creative production and dramatic performances. These balancing activities with their alternating rhythms (Forney et al. 1982) can also be found in quite ordinary circumstances which might not be associated with stress reduction: baking bread, polishing a table, scrubbing the kitchen floor and mowing the lawn. There is a need to match high levels of interaction with adults and children in school with low levels of social contact out of school. There is the need to balance the daily hassles of frustrating colleagues and professional communication with supportive friends or relatives and personal talking and listening. Unfortunately there are teachers without close friends or understanding relatives and so if they want to strengthen their interpersonal resources out of school they must look elsewhere.

There are several ways of meeting people with whom you can share personal talking and listening. You should look for courses or workshops which are concerned with relationships or counselling or groupwork. These will probably provide opportunities to talk about important personal issues and to express feelings which are tightly controlled in school. Exactly who you talk to is not the most important consideration. What is essential is that you find an individual or a group of people with whom you feel comfortable to just be yourself, able to say what you want to say without feeling judged or criticized. The benefit of this kind of experience has been well expressed by one of my students:

> For me the course couldn't have come at a more appropriate time. Just before the course had begun I had failed to get a job which I really wanted in a school where I would really like teaching. When the course started I was finding it very difficult, having stayed in the school, to accept the changes which were beginning to take place. Also at this time I felt under-valued and in a sense very much a failure. My anger was being futher influenced by often being told what an excellent classroom teacher I was. As a result at school I became quite cynical and probably wasn't always the best person to be around.
>
> Having the support of other colleagues on the course and being able to share in some of their disappointments, etc., helped me eventually to come to terms with things. Much of the course also helped me to clarify a great deal of my previous understanding and with time this certainly contributed to the rebuilding of my self-confidence and eventually my self esteem.
>
> I have now managed to achieve many of the objectives which I set out at the beginning of the course.

You may also feel the benefit of expressing your feelings in writing, as the following letter to me suggests. It was written in response to my invitation to a group of headteachers before a workshop to tell me about their work pressures, stress reactions and coping strategies:

> After four years as deputy head I was appointed headteacher of the school. I was naturally looking forward to my new role and felt both excited and anxious for the future. The initial

honeymoon period lasted for about eight weeks. By the end of my first term I was beginning to believe I had made a terrible mistake in leaving the classroom. It is a view I hold to this day.

The question is – why just two terms later do I feel like this? Possibly, the answer lies in the fact that I loved teaching and received tremendous pleasure from my work. Sadly, I do not receive the same job satisfaction from being a headteacher. I often feel as though I have been tricked!

Now you know how I feel about the job – let me state briefly my sources of stress.

First, I find the apathy and poor organization of certain teachers very difficult to live with. I worry about it during school but even more so at home. I often think about their classes and feel angry that the children are not actively involved in their own learning. I attempted to cope with this worry by asking primary advisors to view the classes. I was concerned that it was my own standards, set too high, that was really the problem. The advisors agreed with my analysis and unfortunately could offer very little practical help. I now teach regularly in both classes and after particularly difficult days I return home in a very bad mood. My half-an-hour drive does help release some tension!

Second, throughout my time as deputy head I fostered close relations with parents and school. The school is on a large council housing estate and plays a key role in the community. One aspect of the role of the head that I do enjoy is the contact with parents and supporting agencies. However my parents, with the many social pressures that bear upon them, can be easily upset and I usually receive the full force of their verbal aggression. I know it's ridiculous but I worry about the comments they make.

I often discuss the problems of the day with my husband and this certainly helps. However some days, when I've raced from classroom to office to assembly hall and dealt with cut knee, broken window and social worker and then been called an uncaring snob!, I think to myself is it worth it?

Well, you tell me – is it?

Yours sincerely

PS I feel a lot better after writing this letter!

Assertiveness training

You could also benefit by being with a group of people who are learning to use the skills of assertiveness. In your assertivenes training you may be encouraged to consider why you have become non-assertive and you may find the following analysis helpful:

Fear of unpleasant consequences from assertion. (Anxious about saying No, afraid of an argument.)

Perceiving situations or other people as threatening. (Being unsure of your ability, adopting a 'low' profile.)

Failing to think rationally about yourself. (Freqently comparing yourself unfavourably to other people.)

Confusing assertion and aggression. (Being unduly deferential and apologetic to avoid being seen as aggressive.)

Failing to develop assertive skills. (Being encouraged to behave non-assertively.)

Equating non-assertion with politeness. (Keep quiet rather than disagree with someone else.)

Confusing non-assertion with helpfulness. (Not always helpful, reverse may be true.)

(Back and Back 1982)

You will also be encouraged to practise assertiveness skills whenever you perceive an appropriate opportunity. Some of the most useful approaches are:

1 Standing up for your rights:
   - Making complaints
   - Refusing requests
   - Giving opinions
   - Refusing to be put down.
2 Expressing positive feelings:
   - Telling someone you appreciate them
   - Giving compliments
   - Receiving compliments without embarrassment
   - Starting conversations.
3 Expressing negative feelings:
   - Showing annoyance
   - Showing hurt.

For some colleagues a particular difficulty is expressing rights and positive and negative feelings in staff meetings. If you are like your colleagues in this respect you may welcome the following recommendations for contributing assertively to meetings:

1 Keep your contributions short.
2 Avoid interrupting others.
3 Do not let others interrupt you.
4 Do not wait until the last few minutes to make your contribution.
5 Use eye contact.
6 Keep your non-verbal behaviour assertive.

When you have been practising these recommendations as often as you find practicable you will begin to use to good effect phrases such as:

I believe . . .
I would like . . .
I am good at . . .
This is how I see the situation . . .
Wait a minute, let me deal with one point at a time . . .
I understand that the other arguments are . . .
Let me remind you of the issue before us . . .
I appreciate your point, but I still want to . . .
You could be right; please say more about it . . .
Can you give me an example?
I'd like you to be more specific . . .
Tell me what you expect of me, and I'll do the same for you . . .
Are you really saying . . .
Tell me about . . .
I feel . . .
I intend . . .
This is how I see you . . .

You will probably be encouraged to become more assertive with yourself as well as with other people so that you take the positive decisions and actions which will strengthen your coping strategies. The following report is a warming account of such a development which I want to share with you. It was a wonderful boost to my coping resources.

> I was suffering from blinding headaches and dramatic mood swings, as well as other symptoms or feelings less easy to describe.
>
> I felt myself becoming more and more isolated, trapped and frustrated by these problems and managed to summon up the courage to consult my doctor. Although she was helpful, referring me to the Hospital Neurological unit, I found it very difficult to accurately describe how I was feeling.
>
> I now realize I was suffering from the negative aspects of stress. My teaching was stagnant and uninspired. I was bitter about lack of promotion and the increasing demands of administration on my time. Many of my contempories from University, whom I didn't consider any brighter or better qualified than myself, appeared to be in happier, better paid, less demanding and perhaps less important professions. These factors were combining to produce my stress reactions of headaches, mood swings and isolation. I had to break out of this destructive circle. My stress reactions had me

confused and depressed, which made me more unhappy in my teaching, in turn producing stronger reactions.

I made a conscious decision to pull my teaching back into line, preparing better lessons, researching new resources, marking more frequently for a full academic year and then I would review the situation and my feelings about the profession. I also applied successfully for a place on the Staff Management in Secondary Schools Further Professional Studies course, which revitalized the creative side of me and convinced me that my future lies in teaching.

Together with improving my teaching I became more involved in leisure pursuits. I played football twice a week and the band I play with became more active by both playing live and recording more often. These coping strategies, together with a new approach to the pressures of teaching have restored my positive attitude and my conviction that I can develop within the profession.

Following this review and change of self perception by means of cognitive appraisal and reorganization (Fontana 1989:63), this teacher was also encouraged by me to become more assertive in tackling his work pressures more directly to reduce them at source by considering 'direct-action' recommendations to help him and his colleagues develop school-based strategies and actions. These recommendations are presented in the next chapter, which is concerned with the strengthening of organizational resources at the whole school, department and team levels.

12

RECOMMENDATIONS FOR STRENGTHENING ORGANIZATIONAL RESOURCES

Teachers have made many recommendations for the improvement of the management and administrative systems of their schools and of the services provided by their LEAs. Their main proposals are: effective selection procedures; induction programmes for all staff; the expansion of staff development and management-training opportunities; more support from their colleagues and more effective management of meetings, teamwork, curricular and organizational change, pupil behaviour and stress reduction programmes. These items will therefore provide the frame of reference for my discussion in this chapter of the actions to be taken to strengthen organizational resources. I will also emphasize the importance of appraisal for stress management. The first concern to be considered is the improvement of staff selection.

STAFF SELECTION

Staff selection is a vital task for management. It is the first crucial step in providing and promoting equal opportunities for staff development. It is essential if human-resource management is to be successful in school. Achieving good practice for governors, officers, headteachers and deputies in the management of selection should have a top priority rating, not only because of the widely held perception that too few women and teachers from ethnic minorities are achieving senior positions, or because the contraction of promotion opportunities is keeping staff in the same school for much longer periods of time, or because salaries are the biggest item in a school's budget. There are considerable human costs which can include stress for the person appointed and for his or her colleagues if selection procedures are faulty. So, effective selection is my first recommendation for strengthening organizational resources for stress management.

Mistakes in appointing staff will probably never be totally eliminated, but the chances of appointing an unsuitable head or teacher can be reduced by following a series of stages rather than relying on personal prejudices, eccentric hunches or by making decisions on 'gut feel' within minutes of starting an interview (Courtis 1988). Each of the stages is significant in determining the final decision for the appointment. These interdependent stages are:

1 Analysis of the needs of the organization.
2 Analysis of the tasks performed by the post-holder, leading to the preparation of the job description.
3 Analysis of the personality, qualifications, training, experience, skills and abilities of the person most likely to meet the requirements of the post, i.e. the person specification.
4 Preparation of the advertisement, which should be a brief summary of the job description and person specification. The complete description and specification should be sent to enquirers about the post. In this way some self-guidance takes place if some teachers decide that the post is not suitable for them. This makes the next stage more manageable.
5 Longlisting and shortlisting now take place using information supplied by the candidates and their referees. A structured questionnaire should be used for taking up references based on the job description and person specification, which should also be sent to the referee.
6 Interviewing in which all the people involved (interviewers and interviewees) are well prepared for their respective contributions.
7 Decision-making in relation to the job description and person specification rather than a comparison of the candidates. Disappointed external candidates are grateful for feed-back on the reasons for their non-appointment and on their interviewing style. The internal candidates who are not appointed need more than one post-interview session to cope effectively and productively with their disappointment.
8 Analysis of the interviews by the interviewers and possibly by the interviewees.
9 Follow-up of the person appointed by regular review interviews using the job description as the initial framework.

If these eight steps are integrated into a school's selecion programme the three conditions which are essential for the improvement of selection and interviewing skills will be fulfilled. These three vital requirements are:

1 Interviewers should know how to prepare a job description and a person specification.
2 Interviewers should know how to assess the key factors in the candidates by the use of a systematic interview.

3 Interviewers should be aware of the importance of regularly reviewing the effectivenes of their selection procedures.

Interviewers should know how to prepare a job description

The preparation of a job description and a person specification is
necessary for the selectors and for the guidance of potential candidates.
The job description and person specification should give potential
applicants the information needed for their decision whether to apply
or not. They should include up-to-date, realistic and detailed information about the purpose, scope, duties and responsibilities of the
vacant post and the knowledge, experience, skills and abilities required
to be a successful staff member after appointment.

The information from which a job description is prepared can be
obtained in several ways. It can be sought in an exit interview with the
person whose departure is causing the vacancy. It can be obtained from
discussions with a number of people who are holding appointments
similar to the one which is to be made. Useful guidelines for the
preparation of a job description have been provided by Humphrey
(1983:878). He believes that the following items are essential 'no matter
what level of appointment is being considered':

1 Job title
2 Name of department
3 Accountability: the job title of the person to whom the job holder is
   responsible
4 Main job functions
5 Responsibilities for people and/or equipment.

Additional items are required when considering managerial, super-
visory or technical positions. These include:

6 Limits of authority – particularly in relation to spending money
7 Levels of contact – this is of special importance in a post with
   working relationships outside the organization.

Interviewers should know how to prepare a person specification

When the job description has been written it should be used in
preparing the person specification. This delineates the qualifications,
specific skills and knowledge, experience, training and personal attributes of the person most likely to meet the requirements and demands
of the post. These categories can be qualified by identifying those that
are essential or desirable for a particular job. The final category –

personal attributes – should now be receiving more attention in appointments for a number of reasons, one of which has been identified by Humphreys: 'The impact of the new individual on an existing work group and vice versa can be vital in many situations. Some attempt must be made to analyse the chemistry of the situation.' (Humphreys 1983:881)

More attention should also be given to another personal attribute, that is the stress-management strategies which are essential for management positions. Humphreys again singles this attribute out for particular attention: 'The question of stress and the individual's capacity to absorb stress is very important especially at certain decision making levels.' (p. 881)

When the person specification and job description are complete they can be used in the advertisement for the post. When the shortlist has been prepared by scrutinizing the application forms, CVs, and/or letters of application, the job description and person specification can also be used to guide the questions which are asked during the interview. If the interview is conducted on this framework it will follow the second of my three recommendations for the improvement of selection skills.

Interviewers should know how to assess the key factors in the candidates by the use of a systematic interview

The purpose of the interview is not only to confirm what has been written on the application form. The interview should provide an opportunity to amplify this information and to find out about the important but less tangible factors of motivation, attitudes and expectations. These aspects of personality can be explored in a reasonably satisfactory manner if the interviewers pay attention to the main principles of successful interviewing which have been identified by experienced practitioners. These guidelines may be very briefly summarized as the eight points of a satisfactory interview:

1 The chairperson of the interviewing panel clearly introduces the members.
2 The purpose of the interview is stated, for example, 'The aim of our interview is for us to gain more information about you and to tell you about the school so we can decide if you would be successful and happy working in this environment'.
3 Rapport is established in an atmosphere of informality in a private comfortable room in which telephone calls and other interruptions are avoided. After the introduction the interviewers begin discussing an interesting topic from the application form.

145

4 All questions are asked in a manner which encourages the applicant to talk freely. Questions that evoke a 'yes' or 'no' answer are not helpful. The interviewers should not feel it is necessary to speak if the applicant pauses. The interviewers' silence implies that more information is needed and given time the interviewee usually supplies it.
5 The candidate should be listened to attentively and should not be interrupted.
6 He or she should do most of the talking which occurs in the interview.
7 When the interview is being ended the candidate should be given some indication of future action so that he or she is not left 'hanging in the air' wondering what happens next.
8 As soon as the candidate has left the room the task of evaluating the information should be undertaken. If notes have not been taken a summary of the information should be written into the framework of the job description and person specification.

These eight recommendations are concerned with the three essential phases of successful selection interviewing. These are:

Opening
Continuing
Closing.

In opening the interviewer should attempt to put a candidate at his or her ease and to establish rapport. The right approach is to show consideration (Humphrey 1983:888) through the administrative arrangements and physical setting as well as the interaction between interviewer and interviewee.

In continuing the interview well the importance of framing the questions in the right way cannot be over-stated. This point has been emphasized by the recruitment consultant John Courtis (1988:81) 'It is terribly easy to ask people whether they have done something or whether they have experience of X and Y. That leads straight into yes/ no responses.' Instead he suggests the use of beginning questions with 'how, what, when, where, who and why?'.

In closing the interview Humphrey recommends that a positive approach must be taken and the candidate made aware of the position, for example, she or he will be told the outcome after the last interview or by telephone the next day.

When the task of assessing the information has been completed the interviewers should follow my third recommendation for the improvement of selection skills.

Interviewers should be aware of the importance of regularly reviewing the usefulness and limitations of selection interviews

They will be able to carry out this interview evaluation if they use a checklist of the various aspects of an interview which require attention if it is to be successful. There are a number of questions which are relevant for this purpose:

1 How well did the interviewers receive the interviewee and put him or her at his ease at once?
2 How successfully did the interviewers open the interview? Did they get to the important topics quickly?
3 How successful were the interviewers in moving from one topic to another? Did they direct the conversation unobtrusively? Did they prevent the interviewee wasting time? Did the changes of subject seem abrupt?
4 How successful were the interviewers in closing the interview? Did they close as soon as all the necessary business had been completed? Did the close appear natural and satisfactory to the interviewee? Did it seem abrupt?

The effectiveness of the selection procedures in school can also be assessed by reviewing the progress of the person appointed. This is a significant aspect of the second vital task of human-resource management: induction.

INDUCTION

The link between selection and induction is important and if it is weak the advantages of improvements in the selection process may be lost. Induction, which should be regarded as a key organizational resource, is the process of introducing the new employee to the organization and the organization to the employee. It begins at appointment with introductions to future colleagues, the provision of information about the organization and its departments and about local environmental facilities such as accommodation. This introductory phase of induction continues before the person starts work. A letter of introduction and welcome is an essential and effective part of the process of familiarization with the new role. This essential letter should be followed up by sending the minutes of all subsequent team and departmental meetings.

The process continues as soon as the newcomer takes up his or her appointment. This is necessary for new appointments at all levels of responsibility. It is helpful to set up a formal induction course through which new members of staff learn the policies and systems of the organization. Humphrey (1983) suggests that the best basis from which to start the induction process is the question: what does the newcomer want or need to know? He recommends that a programme of induction must cover such matters as conditions of employment, departmental information, general health and safety. He further recommends that the organizers of these programmes remember that newcomers will find it difficult to assimilate a mass of information at one sitting and a suitable time-scale should be devised.

The value of a successful induction course in the development of school-based coping strategies for staff can be observed in the following statements written by newly appointed staff in a comprehensive school in response to the question: 'Could you briefly outline what you think you have gained from the induction course which will enable you to function more effectively in your present post?'. I asked this question after I was invited to be the external evaluator of the course and I summarized the information given in the evaluation questionnaire and presented it to course members at the end of the first term in school. Their answers to the above question indicated that the course had enabled them to:

1 Gain confidence through knowing more about the school and how it functions
2 Understand how decisions are arrived at in school
3 Be clear as to who was responsible for what
4 Understand each deputy's area of responsibility
5 Know which staff to approach about a specific problem
6 Have a working knowledge of the pastoral system
7 Feel encouraged to make use of information slips, interim reports, etc.
8 Have an increased store of ideas and ways of dealing with kids and situations
9 Have a greater knowledge of what help and advice is available
10 Have a better idea of what is expected with regard to reports and assessments
11 Have more understanding of some of the work and responsibility that go towards higher-scale posts
12 Have a better appreciation of how the adminstrative organization functions both in theory and practice
13 Appreciate the complexity of the financial administration in the school
14 Know the basic history of the school
15 Have a better idea of the catchment area
16 Know where to go for assistance and advice about the potential development of my own subject.

The support for newcomers should include a letter of introduction and welcome written by the appropriate head of department, pastoral-team leader or member of the senior management team. The following letter was written by the deputy head of a comprehensive school and I have included it because it indicates the importance of induction into the tutor's role:

Dear ——

I look forward to working with you next year and will give you as much help and *support* as possible in carrying out your duties as form tutor. (In this respect I also speak for my assistant.) At some time or other all teachers experience problems: it should *never* be a sign of weakness to seek advice. Form tutoring can be very rewarding but equally demanding. As a family man with a wife and three young children I am well aware, however, of the demand made by commitments outside school.

Your year head has already forwarded, or given to you, some suggestions for tutor work, which are intended to form the basis of an induction course for the remainder of the year. Much of it is self-explanatory, but ample guidance will be provided in the use of materials, at the start of term and periodically, thereafter. You must, of course, feel free to complement the materials with your own ideas.

During the first few days of term it might be helpful for us to meet frequently for *short periods of time* in order to clarify points. Previous experience indicates the benefits of this to new members of staff who, by necessity, must assimilate very rapidly a lot of information about the school and its routines. Established tutors will also be only too pleased to help you settle into the school.

I look forward to seeing you on 1st September and take the opportunity to express the hope that you have a very successful term. Enjoy the remainder of the holiday!

Best wishes

The initial letter should be followed up by sending the minutes of all subsequent departmental and tutors' meetings so that the new teacher begins to get a clearer view of the academic and pastoral aspects of a teacher's role in the school.

The importance of successful adjustment facilitated by a sound induction programme for experienced staff and probationary teachers has been clearly presented by Northamptonshire LEA in its staff-development programme:

The first months or year for a teacher taking up a senior post in a new school can be just as testing and just as worrying as for the new probationer. So much is expected of the person that little, if any, allowance is made for the problems of adjustment to a new school climate, to a new set of procedures, to a new team of colleagues, nor, indeed, to a new pupil population. What we should be concerned with is the organization's effectiveness and this cannot be severed from the well-being of the individual. The sooner the individual is working to full and effective capacity, the sooner he is achieving satisfaction from doing his work well, then the better for the school and all those in it. There should, therefore, be a carefully thought out programme of induction for every new member of staff.

It is also important to acknowledge that effective induction pro-grammes are needed for part-time and supply staff. Some insight into the needs of the latter can be gained from the following report of an interview with a supply teacher in her school conducted by one of my students:

Until six years ago, she was an HoD, so the stresses she encountered and the coping skills she employed serve as useful pointers to me when preparing work for supply staff. She suggested:

1 Being a supply teacher was in practice starting a new career and quite different from her previous teaching.
2 Confidence in the classroom had to be re-established.
3 The pupils had changed in outlook over the six years.
4 She had changed.
5 Clearly, supply teachers, like students, are fair game for pupils who like to test them out.
6 A different class each lesson and a fresh set of faces means that a new relationship, on a temporary basis, has be to be forged as frequently as every forty minutes.
7 The lack of specialist subject knowledge by supply teachers is not always fully appreciated by staff or pupils.
8 The behavioural and ability level of the class needs determi-nation and consideration.
9 Work set is sometimes woefully inadequate, overdemanding or – if the supply teacher is fortunate – quite suitable.

All newcomers would probably find it helpful to have similar interviews. If these interviews are held regularly and if in them the newcomer's achievements and problems are discussed positively in a supportive manner a secure basis for the next vital task of the effective management of human resources has been established: appraisal.

APPRAISAL

These types of review interviews are being offered in a growing number of schools by means of structured staff appraisal programmes which are based on regular interviews with a senior member of staff. One framework for these interviews and appraisals is the teacher's job description, which should be accurate and up-to-date. These regular reviews provide good opportunities for the satisfaction of important teachers' needs which include: knowing what is expected of them; having feedback about how their work is evaluated; being able to discuss their strengths and weaknessess objectively and constructively; feeling valued by receiving recognition for effort as well as for achievement; being aware of personal and professional growth and identification of training needs.

Appraisal also provides valuable opportunities for satisfying crucial organizational needs. These are:

1 Assessment of past and present performance and prediction of future contributions from each member of staff
2 An overview of current and potential skills, resources and capabilities available for human resource management in the organization to meet present and future challenges
3 Identification of training needs.

These opportunities to enhance and promote individual and organizational development by using a review interview can only be fully achieved by optimum preparation. Helpful guidelines have been offered by Warwick (1983:12):

The interviewee needs to:

- be given at least one week's notice of the meeting
- be reminded of its purpose
- be asked to think back over all aspects of his work during the period under review
- select areas that he feels to have been particularly worthwhile or unsuccessful in relation to previously set targets
- consider the contributing factors behind both the above
- suggest areas in which in-service training might be helpful
- prepare targets for the next period.

The interviewer should prepare himself/herself by re-considering

- the job description
- the targets agreed at the previous review meeting
- previous meetings both formal and informal during the review period.

Warwick has offered guidelines to good practice for review interviews, which should be:

- regular
- informal
- frank
- two-way
- individual
- confidential
- positive
- constructive
- productive
- supportive.

Successful interviews begin well, continue well and end well. They begin, as I have emphasized with selection interviewing, with the interviewer putting the interviewee at his or her ease and by establishing rapport. The right approach again is to show consideration by careful attention to the administrative details and a physical setting which is free from distraction and interruption as well as the interpersonal interaction.

This good beginning can be continued by 'keeping to the agenda': the job description, the targets set at the previous review meeting, achievements and failures and the reasons for them, the agreement of future objectives and training if appropriate.

A good interview ends well. Both interviewer and interviewee are satisfied that:

- all aspects of the staff member's work have been discussed
- an overall evaluation has been agreed
- objectives/targets have been agreed for the next review period
- training and other resources where necessary have been offered to achieve these goals.

These recommended guidelines strongly suggest that to prepare for, conduct and conclude appraisal interviews requires a high level of managerial competence. Appropriate training in coaching and counselling skills would be a valuable resource for heads and senior staff who would like to develop their skills of staff appraisal.

Another skill which is required for effective appraisal is classroom observation, which is 'one key part of gathering information about teachers' teaching' (National Steering Group 1989:14). Grice and Hanke (1990) have warned against some of the problems which may arise in this type of appraisal. They note that an observer/appraiser may disturb patterns of relationships between teacher and pupil and between pupils themselves. Any observation or even a number of obversations may be an unrepresentative sampling of teacher and pupil behaviour. They refer to one of the 'more sinister aspects of teacher appraisal' which is revealed in the DES (1985) publication *Better Schools*: 'appraisal should lead to the most promising and effective teachers being identified for timely promotion, with those encountering professional difficulties being promptly identified for appropriate couselling, guidance and support, and where such assistance does not restore performance to a satisfactory level with the teacher concerned being recommended for retirement or dismissal' (DES 1985, Para 180).

Grice and Hanke believe that this approach to appraisal would not inspire the confidence or the trust which are so essential for the successful use of appraisal by staff.

Another prerequisite for effectively implementing the regulations announced by the Education Secretary in December 1990, that from September 1991, every teacher in England and Wales will have their performance appraised every two years, is satisfying the staff-training needs which have been identified by classroom observation and a subsequent appraisal interview. This is firmly linked with a fourth factor for successful implementation, that is, putting appraisal in the framework of the school's integrated staff-development policy. I have already suggested that selection should dovetail into induction, which should lead to appraisal by means of the review interview in the induction programme. And training objectives for staff and school should be focused by appraisal.

The identification of professional development objectives by appraisal and the achievement of them by different kinds of training can be accomplished with the help of colleagues. Here is an example presented by a head of department and also one of my Bristol University course members:

> During the last academic year in the writer's school, a group of teachers, from a wide range of subjects, formed a self-support group. Their aim was to assist each other in the development of classroom skills. Since the classroom is a major source of stressful situations, this seemed a commendable scheme in the fact that it was initiated by themselves and not from senior management. The group members attended each others' lessons as observers and, using a previously drawn up format for classroom teaching, commented instructively on each others' methods and development over the course of the year. Members of the group commented on the following benefits they felt they had received:
> (a) identifying skills in others absent in themselves
> (b) becoming aware of pressures faced by teachers in other subjects

    (c) becoming aware of the change in pupils' attitudes with subject

    (d) being able to offer and accept advice from colleagues in a non-critical atmosphere

    (e) having a feeling that others were interested in your work

    (f) the development of respect, confidence and trust in each others' views and feelings related to their school work.

The positive nature of this group started, because of all the benefits gained from it, can only be fully appreciated by those who took part. It would seem from their comments that many of the benefits not only made them more effective teachers, but gave some degree of release from stress.

In this head of department's school not all his colleagues became involved in this type of appraisal which had the unexpected benefits of being a support group and of helping with stress management. Other evaluation programmes have used a whole-school approach which involved all members of staff. One of these developments has been carefully documented by the initiator of the review programme – Peter Thompson, former head of Wheatcroft School Scarborough. He and the staff wrote a brief report of their work after it had been in operation for four years (Thompson 1987).

He argues that a whole-school approach to appraisal should be 'school initiated and self-generating'. For the procedure to be effective 'the whole staff will need to be involved'. The areas of the school for review by staff should be decided upon by staff from the following list: (1) aims, (2) building and general environment, (3) children, (4) curriculum, (5) ethos, (6) finance and resources, (7) governors, (8) headteacher, (9) home, school and community, (10) liaison, (11) non-teaching staff, (12) organization, (13) post-holders, (14) staff development, (15) teacher appraisal. Each of these areas was discussed in turn by using the Spring term for discussion and the Summer and Autumn terms to implement all the recommendations. Two half-hour sessions during the week whilst the head took the school for Assembly/Hymn Practice and a further hour after school each week were used for discussions, which were focused by having no more than five statements for each area, for example:

8 *Headteacher*

    (a) The headteacher should visit each class every day and speak to members of staff individually

    (b) The headteacher should spend part of each day teaching

    (c) The headteacher should take steps to ensure that he shows an

active interest in the professional development, advancement and personal welfare of staff
(d) Parents feel at ease when they visit the school.

But for teacher appraisal (number 15 on the list) the framework for the staff discussions was changed. Instead of the statements, a brief policy paper was prepared which included the following recommendations:

1 Teacher appraisal should be seen as an extension of the school self-evaluation process. Teaching staff with the experience of discussing areas within the school will approach appraisal with less apprehension.
2 If it is seen to be a means of improving the quality of education, through the development and improvement of teacher skills, then it has every chance of being successful.
3 Until headteachers are appraised, the appraisal of teaching staff will not be acceptable.
4 Before appraisal can take place, all teaching staff will require clearly defined job descripions.
5 Areas of appraisal will, in the main, fall into two categories: the interview and classroom observation, and in the case of the head-teacher, observation of his duties over an agreed period.

Four years after its inauguration the School Self-Evaluation project had covered ten of the original fifteen areas for review. It was anticipated that the remaining areas would be completed within the next eighteen months. At the four-year stage the overall conclusion of the staff was:

To sum up we all feel that it has been a helpful and worthwhile exercise. We have learned more about ourselves and our colleagues and we feel we have been able to clarify a common philosophy for the school to work in. We are well aware there are, and will be, areas of weakness where discussion is needed in relation to personalities, but surely to be able to discuss one's professional aims and objectives with one's colleagues in a rational manner is part of our development as professional teachers.

This report of school self-evaluation strongly demonstrates in my view the crucial importance of having staff appraisal clearly within the framework of a whole-school approach to staff development. Other writers have also recently emphasized their agreement with this proposition. The book by joint authors Pratt and Steyning (1989) and that edited by Wilson *et al.* (1989) have given several strategies for achieving the purpose of an appraisal scheme, which is that appraisal should be a tool for professional development (McMahon 1989).
    It is thus essential in my view that training should follow appraisal

and be regarded as the linked next step in an integrated staff-development programme.

TRAINING

It is important for all members of staff that the appraisal system is linked to the in-service training provision so that appropriate opportunities are offered for continuing professional development. This linking is particularly significant for those members of staff who because of contraction of promotion opportunities are now feeling 'trapped' in their present posts and are frightened that their job prospects may not improve. These career-development problems are urgently in need of attention and they continue to be a major concern for the teachers on my management courses.

One of my students recently set out her views on the importance of promoting staff development through training and how she has been helped to articulate her professional objectives and to begin to achieve them:

> In examining the training provisions I would recommend as a component of a staff development programme, I can relate this to my personal needs and systematically plan the way forward in terms of my career. The aims of a staff development programme in providing opportunities for training would be:
>
> To provide continuing development of the professional knowledge, skills and commitment of staff and student teachers.
>
> To encourage individual teachers to plan their careers and to identify and exploit career opportunities.
>
> To clarify the staff's awareness of the school's philosophy, aims and objectives and, through the above, to improve the education of pupils.
>
> In order to achieve these aims, information, advice and support must be readily available to the teachers either through individual, small-group or whole-school involvement. This will include:
>
> The availability of a professional tutor for all members of staff to discuss issues such as the development of classroom management and control skills, opportunities to observe colleagues or visit other schools, discussion of INSET and career opportunities and help with letters of application and interview techniques.
>
> The accessibility of information relating to courses, secondments, current educational issues, training opportunities, etc.

An open invitation to join working parties related to school policies.

Faculty in-service training with head of faculty taking the responsibility for developing individual teacher's in-service needs.

Year team in-service training where year heads encourage the development of the team's pastoral skills.

Management in-service training for heads of year/faculty and senior managers.

Whole-school in-service training including staff meetings and conferences.

I feel that I can use the course as a good model for training within a staff development programme as it has set up the following opportunities for me personally:

1 I have been encouraged to form professional links with the head of a local special school and the deputy head of a comprehensive school, both of whom could now take on the role of professional tutor.

2 By considering the training needs of teachers in school, I am now more aware of my own personal needs.

3 By meeting other teachers on the course and exchanging views with them, I realize that I am not alone in feeling isolated. A support network now exists with additional advice and encouragement available from the tutor.

4 I can refer to the course in my letters of application as an example of my personal attempts to remain in touch with the changes brought about by the Education Reform Act.

5 I have been encouraged to think more clearly about, where do I go from here? and what are the factors involved in making this decision?

6 I have received help in the processes of job applications, interviews, etc.

This last opportunity on her list has been offered by means of group discussion, role-playing and practice interviews. But I also offer guidelines on 'the skills of interviewees', and as they could provide material for INSET they are given here:

Training for interviews

My purpose is to formulate a few guidelines to help interviewees. Whilst 'experienced campaigners' may consider some of the comments trivial, they may also be able to make direct use of others. Interviewees should bear in mind that the interview is a conversation aimed at a particular objective.

Pre-interview preparation

When you are shortlisted for a post it is essential that you are fully prepared for the coming interview. You must ask yourself what the panel will be looking for. Most of this information should be given in the job description; and a careful reading of these details can often reveal more than is at first apparent.

An appraisal of one's own abilities and experience is important and you are advised to keep an accurate copy of the information given on your application forms together with a carbon copy of your letters of application. Far too often a candidate is unable to answer questions on a particular topic of which he or she had claimed, in the letter of application, to have had experience. Apart from this, some weeks may elapse after the application has been submitted before the interviews are held. These copies can then become essential as memory aids.

The interview

Although this section is primarily concerned with the formal interview, it is essential to appreciate that the whole procedure of interviewing begins when you enter the school. It must also be remembered that, at this stage, possible future colleagues will begin to form impressions of you as a potential member of the department/team rather than as a name on an application form. In these informal sessions, as in the formal interviews, many interviewers are susceptible to the first impressions made by the candidate, who can easily appear to be over-confident or over-anxious.

The questions

Certain standard questions are asked in nearly all interviews: they include:

Why did you apply for this post?
Why do you think you are suited for the post
If you are appointed to this post, how do you think the work content will differ compared with your present post?

In answering questions candidates tend to show two common failings: First they try to assess the question from the panel's point of view and to formulate an answer which they feel the panel would like to hear. Most interviewers are looking for candidates who show that they have thought about their work and who are able to form reasoned opinions. Most interviewers will respect such opinions even if these are contrary to the view they hold themselves. The interviewee must therefore give the answer which she or he thinks to be correct and must support this with an argued case.

Second, they are not prepared to be decisive. The candidate who realizes that he or she has made an error should acknowledge this. On the other hand it must be recognized that hedging the answer with too many qualifications may lead the panel to decide quite wrongly the candidate is not able or willing to make decisions. This factor is particularly relevant to senior posts. If you mishear or misunderstand a question you should ask the interviewers to repeat or rephrase it. On the other hand, if you realize that one of your previous answers has been so badly phrased that it could have given the wrong impression, it should be clarified as soon as possible. Towards the end of the interview, you will usually be given the opportunity to question the panel and to add any information, on topics which have not been covered, which would strengthen the application. You must use this opportunity to the full, if only to clarify any badly answered questions. On the other hand if you have nothing to ask or to add you should say so. Asking questions on trivial matters for the sake of asking questions does not leave a good impression. Questions concerning salaries, removal expenses and housing costs are not trivial.

The internal candidate

If you are an internal candidate applying for a post you may meet problems which are peculiar to your special situation. These mainly arise because you will know and be known by one or more members of the interviewing panel. You may wonder whether there is a need to be interviewed at all. But the interviewers may expect more from you than from an external candidate. It is extremely important for you to ensure that it is a good interview and preparation for this must be sound. It should not be assumed that your 'inside' knowledge will allow any skimping on the preparation. The best method of meeting these problems is to treat the interview as if you were an external candidate.

Follow-up

Whether the application has been successful or not you should try to assess your performance after each interview. The following questions could be used as performance criteria:

Did I talk for too long or too short a period?

Did I possess sufficient knowledge to answer the questions in full?
Was I able to answer the questions concisely?
Were my answers to particular questions given in a logical sequence?
Did I really want the job?

These guidelines for interviewees should provide stimulation for discussion and learning and they should be re-written when they do not match your experience. It is also necessary for you to be aware that preparation for promotion means more than learning a few guidelines for being an effective interviewee. It means analysing very carefully the knowledge and skills which are needed for effective performance of the post you wish to apply for. The required knowledge and skills can be acquired in several ways: reading, and attending courses or self-directed staff development in school to gain experience of the activities which are part of the job you want and to make a realistic appraisal of the pressures experienced by the post-holders. If you can obtain the position of personal assistant or deputy to this senior position you will find more opportunities for identifying these demands and the knowledge and skills which are needed to tackle them effectively.

Training for teamwork

Some of the most important skills you will recognize if you follow these recommendations will be the teamwork skills of communication, co-operation and support. It is therefore an essential training objective that staff-development programmes are organized in school to provide members of senior management, department and pastoral care teams with regular opportunities to learn and to practise these skills.

Considerable thought, time and effort should be given to the development and maintenance of effective teamwork. Training to achieve these goals is now a realistic possibility as there is a considerable fund of information, research and experience, for example about the process of effective team-building, which can be achieved in four stages. These are:

Objectives   The objectives of the team should be clearly understood by all members.

Procedure   All team members should be involved in making important decisions.

Process   All team members should be clear about what has to be done, by whom, with what resources and within what time contraints.

Review   The team should review its work regularly as part of a learning and development process.

(Bell and Maher 1986:32)

The first and last of these stages are particularly important in team-building. The setting of objectives is a prime task and carrying them out should be the goal of a properly functioning team. In such a team a number of characteristics can be identified:

1 People care for each other
2 People are open and truthful
3 There is a high level of trust
4 Decisions are made by consensus
5 There is a strong team commitment
6 Conflict is faced up to and worked through
7 People really listen to ideas and to feelings
8 Feelings are expressed freely
9 Process issues (task and feelings) are reviewed.

(Critchley and Casey 1986: 27)

The review stage in team-building is as important as the setting of objectives. This last stage is reached when teams set aside some time regularly in their team meetings to review their success in meeting the nine criteria of an effective team. Such a process review enables a team to monitor its teamwork, to identify its strengths and weaknesses and to work to change the latter. This is essentially the recognition of good practice in the team and sharing it with all the team members.

Meetings

The characteristics which teams show in their development can be most clearly seen in their meetings. Jay has argued that

> In the simplest and most basic way a meeting defines the team. . . . We all know who we are – whether we are on the board of Universal International, in the overseas sales department of Flexitube Ltd, a member of the school management committee, in the East Hampton football team or in Section No 2 of Platoon 4, company B.
>
> (Jay 1976:10)

This awareness of a team which can be enhanced by meetings is strengthened by members developing and sharing a common fund of knowledge, experiences, feelings, making decisions and overcoming problems. This fund can also be thought of as a joint bank account into which members contribute their deposits of time, energy, learning and skills and from which they can make withdrawals on demand. Meetings also encourage teamwork by strengthening commitment to the team's objectives, policies, decisions and actions. Members can become aware of common ownership of problems and procedures in the face to face contact of a meeting.

These advantages of meetings for successful teamwork can only be realized by means of good planning, clearly presented objectives, good organization of the interaction between members, well formulated decisions and actions and follow-up procedures to check the effectiveness of decisions. It is a very important part of the team leader's role to ensure that 'meetings are vehicles for communication and action rather than for confusion and frustration' (Everard and Morris 1985:51). Effective meetings can be achieved but there are important requirements. The first of these is thorough planning. Nine major recommendations have been made by Lambert (1986) for team leaders to follow:

Clearly establish the purpose of the meeting. Is it:
   (a) To identify/solve a problem
   (b) To agree procedures
   (c) To define policy
   (d) To give information
   (e) To seek information
   (f) To make a decision
   (g) To motivate people
   (h) To settle differences?
Clarify objectives
Have clear procedures
Decide who attends:
   (a) as of right as a team member
   (b) as invited participants
   (c) as observers.
Size of meeting:
   (a) large enough to provide necessary experience and discussion
   (b) not so big that it is indecisive and time consuming.
How long should the meeting last?
Agenda:
   (a) Agree upon it in advance and identify major points for discussion
   (b) There is less likelihood of important points being overlooked
   (c) It should be clear and unambiguous.
Minutes:
   (a) Decide who should compile these
   (b) Make provision for identification of action to be taken and individuals to take it
   (c) Decide to whom copies are to be distributed.
Follow-up:

Arrange to check on whether decisions are being implemented by designated person(s).

Successful team meetings require the management of people as well as procedures. Jay (1976: 15) has identified a number of problems concerned with members' behaviour in meetings and put forward recommendations for resolving them. His suggestions are:

1 Control the garrulous. If someone takes a long time and many words to say very little of relevance, the chairperson's sense of urgency should help indicate to them the need for brevity. The manager can also suggest that if they are going to take a long time it might be better for them to write a paper!
2 Draw out the silent. Jay suggests that there are two kinds of silence which require management attention. These are:
(a) the silence of diffidence
(b) the silence of hostility.
The diffident member may have a valuable contribution to make to the discussion but he may be nervous about the reaction of colleagues. The team leader can use eye contact and attention to encourage the member to speak. The silence of hostility, Jay suggests 'is usually the symptom of some feeling of affront'. It is a help to effective teamwork if the feelings of anger are expressed directly rather than maintained as an angry silence.
3 Protect the weak. Junior members (because of inexperience, age, status or job) may have their contributions dismissed by their senior colleagues as not worthy of the team's time and interest. The team leader should commend their contributions 'by taking a written note of a point they make (always a plus for a member of a meeting) and by referring to it again later in the discussion (a double-plus)'.
    The manager can also promote the contribution of the less experienced, younger and junior members by asking for their contributions first before the big guns start firing.

If these recommendations for effective teamwork are implemented in the whole-school policies colleagues will achieve their objectives of communication, co-operation and support. They will then be enabled to share their problems, feelings of anxiety and frustration and strategies in some of their senior management, department and pastoral team meetings.

Dealing with children's misbehaviour

These anxieties, frustrations and problems are often concerned with children's behaviour and help with misbehaviour can make a significant contribution to staff stress management. These difficulties are compounded when teachers are reluctant to discuss their discipline problems with other staff in case they lose face, particularly if they work in schools where they are 'left high and dry trying to work out their own professional salvation on an ad hoc basis' (Farley 1989) and where the management of misbehaviour is perceived by staff as inconsistent, incoherent and usually inadequate.

These worries can be seen in a recommended strategies checklist compiled by a small group of teachers in one of my recent workshops for a whole school staff:

Staff recommended strategies for disruptive behaviour in school

1 Maintain a calm discipline
2 Remove children into another classroom if possible
3 Separate children to a separate table
4 Reason with them about the undesirability of aggressiveness
5 Gear work to suit ability
6 Vary the task set
7 Ensure that a wide range of activities and approaches are used with constant revision
8 Self-evaluate that I dealt with the situation correctly
9 Mentally calm yourself down
10 Consult external agencies
11 Talk to and counsel
12 Behavioural approaches
13 A provision for consistently problematical pupils
14 Structured course/meetings aimed at improving classroom management
15 Share ideas and strategies in a working party similar to the attitudes and behavioural sub-committee set up by our feeder school staff
16 Suitable supply cover
17 Identify non-stressful activities for class and use these when needed
18 Smaller groups per teacher rather than two teachers per class
19 Adopt a stance as relaxed as possible
20 More effective sanctions
21 Avoid unnecessary confrontations
22 More effective back-up facilities
23 Regular discussion with other members of staff
24 An understanding and sympathetic senior management team
25 Set standards and a series of rewards and punishments
26 Decide a policy of priority of jobs for middle managers and alter timetable demands
27 More personal involvement and interest from senior staff.

Table 12.1 Some common behavioural problems: a ready-reference chart

Incident	Possible cause	Suggested action
Your class engages in chatter and uninvited comments or asides.	Release from previous hard-line teacher. Pupils not impressed by you or your lesson.	More discussion, activity. Examine your own attitude and lesson selection and preparation.
Difficult pupil, won't co-operate, becomes aggressive or insolent.	Probably a combination of home, school, social conditions, experience.	Get to know him. Infiltrate, don't victimize. Liaise with other staff.
Pupils seem bored.	School regime? Narrow (exam?) curriculum? Your lessons are dull and pointless.	Not a lot you can do about the regime, but you can revise lessons and teaching methods.

Source: Farley, 1989, p. 10

This list is concerned with individualized classroom approaches and with organizational whole-school strategies. Both are necessary for the effective satisfaction of staff and students' needs. The personal method has been clearly formulated by Farley (1989:32) in a framework which I have abbreviated (Table 12.1).

The importance of training in classroom-management skills has been persuasively advocated by the Elton Committee. In their report they argue that 'there is a high degree of agreement in the literature about the main features of good practice' (DES and Welsh Office 1989:71). These include:

- Making the rules for classroom behaviour clear to pupils from the first lesson and explaining why they are necessary
- Planning and organizing both the classroom and the lesson
- Being aware of and able to control their own behaviour 'including stance and tone of voice'
- Knowing their pupils as individuals
- Being flexible 'to take advantage of unexpected events rather than being thrown off balance by them'. (The examples of flexibility given by the Committee are 'the appearance of a window cleaner or a wasp in the middle of a lesson'!)
- Emphasizing the positive aspects of pupil behaviour and work
- Analysing their own classroom management performance and learning from it. 'This is the most important message of all.'

The contribution of school policies, organization and management are crucial to the successful achievement by staff of these objectives, for example, if staff are nomadic because of their timetable it is sometimes difficult to plan and organize every one of the four or more different classrooms they visit each day!

This whole-school policy perspective has been ably presented by a number of writers including Galloway (1987:115), who has argued that schools and teachers should 'overcome their preoccupation with the behaviour of individual pupils and individual teachers' and should recognize that a whole-school approach to disruptive behaviour is likely to be effective.

Charlton and David (1989) have proposed that a whole-school policy for children's (mis)behaviour should be concerned with classroom incentives and punishments, school philosophy and rules, internal/ external communication systems, staff liaison and pastoral responsibilities, school leadership and management systems, teacher assessment/appraisal and staff development, the curriculum and the school 'climate'.

The Elton Committee in their report (DES and Welsh Office 1989:80) strongly recommended that 'headteachers and teachers should, in consultation with governors, develop whole school behaviour policies which are clearly understood by pupils, parents and other school staff'. The emphasis of the Committee, rightly in my view, was the encouragement of good behaviour. They suggested some ways of implementing the whole-school policies, for example:

- A small number of essential school rules expressed in positive terms wherever practicable
- The rules are applied judiciously and consistently by all members of staff
- The emphasis on the use of rewards for a range of academic and non-academic achievements and on contact with parents should communicate pupils achievements as well as problem behaviour
- Avoiding both the injudicious use of group punishment for infringement of rules where the innocent, as well as the guilty, are punished and public punishment which humiliates individuals.

The Committee also made helpful suggestions emphasizing the importance of the implicit rules of a school which provide opportunities and set constraints on both teacher and pupil behaviour by shaping their interactions each day. The Committee reported:

When we visited schools we were struck by the difference in their 'feel' or atmosphere. Our conversations with teachers left us convinced that some schools have a more positive atmosphere than others. It was in these positive schools that we tended to see the work and behaviour which impressed us most. We found we could not explain these different school atmospheres by saying that the pupils came from different home backgrounds. Almost all the schools we visited were in what many teachers would describe as difficult urban areas. We had to conclude that these differences had something to do with what went on in the schools themselves.

(DES and Welsh Office 1989: 80)

These differences in atmosphere or ethos or school climate are related to what has been called 'the affective curriculum' (Hanko 1989). This is the system of values in the school which is expressed in the quality of the relationships between management and staff, colleagues, teachers and pupils, pupils and teachers and non-teaching staff and amongst the pupils themselves.

Quality is found where these interactions are characterized by support, trust and respect. The Elton Report, again rightly in my view, endorses the pivotal importance of school-based support policies for all members of the school organization as they attempt the task of implementing the Elton recommendations. So, training for staff with the aim of improving classroom behaviour should be based on support, trust and respect and not on a 'narrow interpretation of skills training. It must aim to augment teachers' ability to find their own solutions to the problems they face with their most difficult-to-teach pupils. It needs to have a problem solving consultative framework' (Hanko 1989:140).

The training model needed to implement this approach is very similar to the one I use for staff stress management which will be discussed in the next and final section of this chapter. Hanko suggests that this approach 'requires an in-service coordinator who can arrange for the staff to meet in their schools, pool their expertise and share and develop their understanding in regular workshops' (Hanko 1989:141). This staff development may be initiated by an outside consultant or initiator who 'needs to be well versed in the consultative skills required to work with fellow professionals, understand the difficulties in their work setting and be able to ensure that the (workshop) sessions will cater for both the immediate and long term needs of teachers' (Hanko 1989:143). The consultant is not the 'sole expert' in the group. She or he should pool her or his expertise with that of the staff. The aim of the group, with the consultant's help, is to develop their support and problem-solving skills, which should continue to develop after the consultant has left the group.

A similar approach to training has been used by one of the students on my Bristol staff management course. He and a colleague were the school co-ordinators of PAD (Preventive Approaches to Disruption) programmes (Chisholm *et al.* 1986). They set out the aims of PAD in their introductory paper to their colleagues:

> The PAD course with or without refinements is designed to be interactive – we wish to keep it that way. We have no magic answers. We do not consider ourselves experts. We do feel, however that by meeting as a group and focusing on particular areas we *will* be able to (i) raise our awareness of key issues; (ii) recognize and identify the ways in which we, as teachers, influence pupils' learning experiences and (iii) discover ways which will help us *change behaviour* both in pupils and importantly in teachers. We feel these are the three main aims of the programme. We look forward to your company.

In their introduction they also said that PAD had been strongly recommended by the Elton Report (the Committee included it in their selected bibliography of 'useful in-service training materials'). The PAD materials are divided into three broad areas:

Non-verbal communication
Lesson organization
Management of pupils.

The co-ordinators told their colleagues that in a PAD course there are ground rules 'to provide a framework within which you, as course members, can share your experiences, ideas and difficulties constructively'. These are the suggested ground rules:

- Material contributed by course members is confidential
- Offer alternatives rather than give advice
- Speak for yourself and avoid generalizations
- You have the right to opt out of any activity
- Take responsibility for your own learning
- Develop your skill in listening attentively to each other
- Acknowledge the positives in yourself and others.

These recommended approaches to staff training to help them manage children's behaviour are relevant for also helping them to reduce their occupational stress levels. In this last section of my book I want to present and discuss a case-study of a workshop for staff to give you a practical example of my approach to stress management which might contribute to your INSET.

STRESS MANAGEMENT: CASE-STUDY OF A WORKSHOP FOR STAFF

Training in stress management to strengthen organizational resources in best achieved through whole-school policies. There are several different models of training available and each school should choose that model which is appropriate for the needs of its staff. Both teaching and non-teaching staff should be involved from the beginning of the preparation and planning of the programme. If a school decides to follow the usual pattern of having an INSET day, preparation and planning should start several months before the agreed date. As a case-study I want to discuss one of my recent consultative partnerships with the staff of a Sixth Form College. I was first contacted by the INSET co-ordinator in October to ask if I would take part in an INSET conference the following July. During this first conversation by telephone I asked if a small working party of teaching and non-teaching staff could be formed to plan and manage the conference. I met with them for the first time in January and once more in May in the college. At the first meeting we discussed our objectives for the INSET day and I suggested that it should be thought of as the beginning of the stress-reduction policies in college and not an end in itself. We also discussed a possible programme for the day and I presented copies of the programmes I had used elsewhere. The third important item for discussion was my proposal that a questionnaire be presented to staff inviting them to give us information in response to a number of questions relating to the pressures they were experiencing, how they were reacting to the pressures and what areas of concern should be discussed on the INSET day. The working party agreed to have further discussion on the questionnaire so that we could agree on a final version at our next meeting. The INSET co-ordinator at this meeting told me that he was the head of the English department and would be interested in discussing stress management with the members of his department and making the details of the discussion available for our next meeting and for the INSET day if his team agreed.

Before our next meeting in March he wrote to me:

> I enclose a copy of the English department's minutes of its discussion on stress management. You will notice that given the opportunity to discuss elements of stress within the subject area, people easily identified their concerns. What was interesting, however, was that as discussion progressed there was a realization that many of the pressures yield their own solutions and that we often deliberately create our own stress (in the classroom) because it makes for a more exciting lesson. In other words, I thought that the group moved from a 'negative' to a more

169

'positive' position. I shall be interested to hear your responses. Here are the minutes:

English department: stress management exercise

Discussion began with an analysis of the activities undertaken by the department during the academic year:

September: Enrolment and induction of new students. Preparation of departmental prospectus for next academic year.

October: Open evenings for prospective new students. Progress reports ('Sweep') on new students encountering problems in A-level and one-year courses.

November: Parents' Evening (Lower Sixth and one-year students).

December: Preparation of papers for 'mock' A-level examination. (Between September and December, staff will be updating pre-UCCA/PCAS forms for student references.)

January: 'Mock' examination. (The period the of the 'Mock' examination with its marking and subsequent discussion of student performance was seen as the most demanding time of year.)

February: Parents' Evening (Upper Sixth and one-year students).

March: Second series of progress reports on Lower Sixth and one-year students encountering problems. Lower Sixth reports. Group Orals for GCSE.

April: Internal Moderation of GCSE coursework.

June: Lower-sixth examinations. Parents' Evenings.

July: Completing of first phase of pre-UCCA/PCAS forms.

Activities taking place throughout the year:
1 Marking and assessment of A-level work and GCSE coursework
2 Departmental meetings, formal and informal
3 Interviews with individual students
4 Expeditions.

Pressures identified by the department

English is a heavily subscribed subject with about 500 students pursuing the courses we offer (A-level courses in English Literature and English Language, A/S English, GCSE (Mature) courses in English Language and English Literature and RSA English).

1 Volume of marking and assessment in a subject where 'impression marking' is impossible.
2 Ensuring that the syllabus is completed on time.
3 Pace of change within the subject and the difficulty of obtaining reliable and consistent information from Examination Boards. Examination Moderators are constantly redefining their demands and expectations. GCSE has generated more meetings.
4 Difficulty in finding adequate training time for new syllabuses.
5 Feeling of guilt about unfinished work.
6 Frustration caused by unavoidable absence of students (e.g. Field Trips, Work Experience) and concern about stress upon colleagues in other departments when we 'remove' their students from classes (e.g. for GCSE Orals).
7 Encroachment of other responsibilities outside the classroom.
8 Feelings of being undervalued in the community at large.
9 Part-time staff concerned about missing important information which will be known to full-time staff.
10 Fear that development of staff–student pre-UCCA/PCAS negotiation will reduce teaching time in the future.

Attempts to find solutions

1 Not all stress is negative. The 'creative' stress of engagement with the work and the students is stimulating and enjoyable.
2 We should look for new ploys for new syllabuses (e.g. 'distance' learning). We should reflect on the fact that our responses are conditioned by our own education in a 'tried and tested' examination system and that our worries may be caused by the abolition of O-level and its rigid criteria. New approaches will not be 'alien' after a while and transition is always painful.
3 Try to avoid guilt by setting realistic targets; try to identify one's limitations and decline extra tasks which may cause too heavy a workload.
4 Seek opportunities for appropriate in-service training.
5 Ensure effective communication.
(There was a feeling in the department that a session about 'Managing Change' would be a very useful component of our INSET day on Stress Management.)

At the May meeting we agreed on the objectives for the day as:

1 To enable members of the college staff to achieve a clearer understanding of the signs and causes of stress in themselves

and in others; to develop methods of coping and reducing their own stress and to provide appropriate support for colleagues.

2 To arrive at specific recommendations for beneficial change in working practices within the college.

We agreed on the programme:

Programme

8.55 a.m. Coffee – Staff Dining Room
9.10 a.m. Staff assemble in Library Study Area
9.15 a.m. Background to the conference
Objectives of the day
Introduction of Dr Jack Dunham
9.30 a.m. *Session 1* (Plenary): Jack Dunham
Definitions of stress
What it is; what it isn't
Strategies for reducing stress
Identification of work pressures in college
10.15 a.m. *Session 2* Working parties
(please see below for details of groups and rooms)
Aims of working parties
(a) For your designated area, to move towards a recognition of issues which cause stress in college
(b) To identify effective action for its reduction
(c) To make policy recommendations for a college action plan
11.00 a.m. Coffee – Staff Dining Room
11.20 a.m. *Session 2* (continued)
12.15 p.m. Lunch – Common Room
Wine will be provided
1.15 p.m. *Session 3* (Plenary): Jack Dunham – Library Study Area
How can stress be recognized and therefore reduced?
Ways of coping with stress
2.00 p.m. *Session 4* (Working parties)
(Please see below for details of groups and rooms)
Aims of working parties
(a) To examine possible ways of reducing stress for oneself and one's colleagues
(b) To make policy recommendations for a college action plan
3.15 p.m. Close
Working party leaders are asked to bring recommendations to the Library Study Area.

172

Please note that a summary of recommendations will be published next term.

At the May meeting I found that the working party had produced a different questionnaire from any I had used elsewhere. It was a much improved version and questions 1 and 3 helped me to develop conceptually. The final form of the questionnaire was:

As you know, there will be an INSET Day on Stress Management on Thursday 12th July in response to staff requests. The following questionnaire is intended to help us to create a programme for the day based on colleagues' needs and to enable you to answer freely we are not asking you to put your name to your response. Please answer the questions as fully or as briefly as you wish and return to my pigeon-hole by 3.45 p.m. on Monday 11th June. Thank you in advance for your co-operation.

1 What pressures of your work do you find acceptable and enjoyable?
2 What pressures of your work cause the greatest anxiety/stress/problems?
3 Some of the areas you have identified in Question 2 may be 'non-negotiable' (i.e. contractual); others are 'negotiable'. To help further analysis, please fill in the following table.

	Source of Stress	What do you do about it?	What else can you do?	Is there anything that the college could do?
'Non-negotiable' area				
'Negotiable' area				

4 How do you react if your attempts to reduce pressure are ineffective?
5 Which of the following do you think would merit further discussion and exploration on the INSET day? Please tick the areas which interest you.
(a) Time management
(b) Management of change

(c) Operating in a team
(d) Methods of coping with stress
(e) 'Assertiveness' (i.e. being firm without being aggressive)
(f) Communication
(g) Management of meetings
(h) Managing conflict
(i) Marking
(j) Relationships with students
6 Any further comments?

Only a few days after 11 June I received the completed questionnaires and a letter from the INSET co-ordinator:

I think that fifty-one (out of a possible seventy) responses represents a good cross-section of staff opinion. They are very interesting indeed; needless to say also the questionnaire has provoked a great deal of discussion among the staff. We are going to attempt a resumé for the programme but clearly the information received will form a useful basis for long-term consideration of this area.

The areas which seem to be popular for afternoon discussion are items (a) to (i) in question 5; (j) doesn't seem to be a major worry because it is linked with the 'acceptable' and 'enjoyable' in question 1. It would seem that there should be groups for (a) to (i) in the afternoon and we welcome your suggestion that you be a facilitator for a group considering the reduction of our own stress.

Arrangements for the day are making progress and the whole project is arousing excitement and curiosity.

The information given by staff in their questionnaire responses was also summarized and presented by me in my plenary sessions. The details they reported of their work pressures, stress reactions and recommendations were generally very helpful to me and to the senior management team. As members of staff commented: 'Nobody has asked us these questions before'.

To provide an illustration of the valuable material for stress-management policies which can be made available by a relatively short questionnaire I want to quote one member's responses in full:

1 *What pressures of your work do you find acceptable and enjoyable?*
● Teaching an interesting subject to a lively and responsive group of 16–18 year olds.
● Developing new resources – planning, researching, creating.
● Establishing a good rapport with a group of students.
● Helping students overcome problems/difficulties encountered

in their work (content, approach, etc.) – usually on an individual basis.

- Responding to 'difficult' questions posed by students and com municating complex ideas in a clear and coherent fashion! (Hopefully).
- Parents evenings (mostly) and open evenings.
- Departmental/curriculum meetings with constructive and focused discussion.
- Working on a variety of courses.
- Keeping up to date, learning about new developments in relevant subject areas.

2 *What pressures of your work cause the greatest anxiety/stress/problems?*
The particular nature of our institution (no student more than twenty months from final assessment or exam) needs to be taken into account, for example when planning holidays (very bad this year: cramming in contact-time has I think had a seriously deleterious effect on staff and student morale – people are not machines, and their need for rest and humane *pacing* of their work must be assessed rationally and sympathetically; if the aim is efficiency, this is the way to a *true* efficiency.)
Lessons – teaching A-level and GCSE is very hard, concentrated work, intellectually and emotionally. Comparisons with stress in schools, though salutary, are less relevant than they seem: we do the best we possibly can at *this* level and in *these* circumstances, and it is tiring. Some who have taught in 'difficult' schools say that our challenges are different but in their way equally taxing – I wouldn't know! A genuine pressure is the constant awareness that the College's survival depends on our success in academic results, making subject lessons our *principal* area of work; I think we have a tendency to take this work for granted and that this is dangerous (every innovation takes away time and energy from this central responsibility and the flow of such innovations is a constant worry). For example, this year I have had an A-level class whom I have taught period 6 on Thursday and period 1 and 3 on Friday – convenient for timetable, but not good for students. Thursday 6 in not 'prime time', and in any case it is too close to the Friday lessons; the students are short-changed on Friday because the lessons are shorter in any case and period 1 has often been shortened by the pressures of the preceding tutorial period or assembly. My point is that, whatever arguments could be brought on the other side, the *effect* of this throughout the year has been to make me feel that my class's lessons 'do not matter' as much as they should. They have their 'slot' in the day, but the actual *quality*

of that slot does not seem to matter much compared to the demands of 'college period day'.

Set tutor's role – at registration, the accumulation of duties, trivial in themselves but combining to cause or increase stress (handing out/collecting notes, pursuing absentees, etc. – it seems ridiculous to name these as causes of stress, but in the context of a difficult teaching day they assume an infuriating prominence – this is I suppose, what stress is all about!). Morning registration should be longer, more leisurely; p.m. one seems to evaporate.

Careers Work – despite really excellent support, this is stressful; especially so, surely, for the less experienced? I think it was better when senior staff and experienced people did this work. A sign of pressure here is the fact that some of the references I come across are really not very good (and they go out with spelling mistakes sometimes – a sign of pressure at the final stage?).

Tutorial Period – often causes stress; having to do several things at once; having to support or justify them in face of student scepticism (and remember they are articulate, independent-minded people, some very clever and 19 years old or even more). Sometimes one does not believe in the activities oneself (I know we have to face this – I'm just saying what causes pressure). The fact that no two weeks follow the same pattern is something else you have to think about – in itself, nothing, but in the context of a busy teaching day, stressful.

ROAs – It is stressful to have to take part in a process whose validity you doubt, or whose advantages (there are some) are outweighed by disadvantages. The feeling that one's opinion of them (and I know many sceptics, no enthusiasts) counts for nothing, is frustrating. ROAs take time away from teaching, so one does them as swiftly as possible, knowing that more time should be devoted to them; this adds a sense of *bad faith* to irritation – very stressful. *In fact this feeling that one is not doing properly something whose validity one doubts in any case is, I'm convinced, a major cause of stress in college.* There are so many better ways of using the time and energy. It is very worrying that ROAs will be extended to all students next year: once again teaching efficiency will be threatened, while good academic results will become no less important. For Set Tutors the demands on time and energy will be great – pity those who are both subject tutors and set tutors! Being a set tutor used to be fun and fulfilling – now it has become a draining chore with *overtones* of fun and fulfilment but few steady, consistent satisfactions. Yet it is on this kind of satisfaction that effective pastoral care depends. How ironic that much of the pressure has arisen from the recent *schematization* of what is now deadeningly called 'the pastoral programme'. The pastoral care at the college is still good, and has recently been praised to me by students by contrast with that at other alternative institutions in the area, both maintained and independent; in my gloomy moods I fear that this will not last (a point made very forcibly to me by a recent leaver whose insights I have great respect for). This is all obviously a source of stress.

3 *Some of the areas you have identified in Question 2 may be 'non-negotiable' (i.e. contractual): others are negotiable'. To help further analysis please fill in the following table.*

'Non-negotiable area	My replies here are implied by my comments elsewhere. In general, the college could be less eagerly committed to innovations than it seems to be. I think that there is a problem in showing the staff that their strengths and opinions have been taken account of before a commitment to change or innovation is made – there are many clever people here with much experience of teaching in the sixth form and much knowledge of students in the age group. They need to feel that they matter. This is particularly important at a time of general demoralization in the teaching service.
	I also think that more frequent assemblies should be reintroduced and that more frequent, less formal contact should be established between the executive and the students.
'Negotiable Area'	Negotiable by whom and with whom? (this isn't an aggressive question but an honest one!). I have noticed that when new ideas are put to the staff at meetings they are more and more met not with lively and articulate debate but with a kind of grim resignation that is disturbing. This suggests that the idea of 'negotiation' needs some thought: did we 'negotiate' tutorial period, ROAs (both sources of stress), etc. – and if so, to what extent? I come back to the question of academic results and the assumption that they will remain good if we keep reminding ourselves how important they are – an assumption we all find it comfortable to make. Stress arises from an awareness that *more* is needed: able, intelligent people who are good teachers need to be retained on the staff; matters such as 'revision technique' and the transfer from GCSE to A-level, instead of being hived off

into the pastoral programme, should be entrusted to the departments (i.e. the staff in their capacity as subject teachers) who should be encouraged to work through their own solutions in the light of their professional knowledge; students (who suffer from stress too) should be asked what aspects of the college 'experience' they have found most valuable and which have irritated them – I reckon that most of them would give priority to good, relaxed teaching and good, relaxed pastoral work (though they might not give it that name). We *must* give them what they want and the fear that we may not causes me stress.

4 *How do you react if your attempts to reduce pressure are ineffective?*
Generally, with a sense that it is the causes of stress that need to be dealt with rather than its symptoms. Insomnia, comfort eating, inability to concentrate – yes to all three – what a doleful response! Sometimes a serious regret that I have become a teacher.

Apart from my plenary sessions and my role as facilitator for an afternoon working party I also contributed a booklet of working papers. These included checklists of stress reactions and coping strategies which were used during my interactive plenary sessions, and brief guidelines to provide starting points for the working parties. To illustrate this last point I want to present suggested guidelines for:

- Change management
- Time management
- Assertiveness.

Guidelines for effective change management

1 You and your colleagues need to be informed and consulted about your opinions and feelings and need to be active participants in changes that are affecting your role.
2 You and your colleagues should participate with the head or deputy head or the senior management team, or middle management in working out a careful strategy for change which should be implemented in stages.
3 All of you should be clear about your objectives and agree on realistic targets. When the first targets are achieved ensure that everyone's contribution is appreciated.
4 You should make your training needs known and share your feelings and even your apprehensions if you have any.

5 You should restrict any other changes that are not related to the Reform Act to the absolute minimum.
6 You should share your disappointments if things do not happen as intended in the plans.
7 You should support your colleagues (including the head and management teams) if they need it and let them support you if you need it.

The most important conclusion that I draw from these guidelines is that it is essential for staff to support each other during the process of implementing the Reform Act because they will be fully successful in managing the changes only if they share plans, problems and feelings.

But managing change effectively also requires management action. Plant (1987) has proposed 'six key activities for successful implementation' which are as follows:

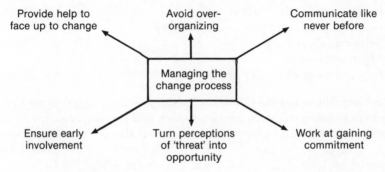

Source: adapted from Plant 1987, p. 32

Figure 12.1 Six key management activities for successful implementation of change

Guidelines for effective time management

The time required for these innovations cannot be extended because of the fixed number of hours specified in each teacher's contract. So, in school, time may be appropriated from non-essential activities as defined by the National Curriculum, such as school visits, and from non-core subjects such as careers and personal and social education. In this way core requirements may be subsidized by non-core hours. Outside school there could be a similar problem of appropriation but in this case the subsidizing will be from family time and the time previously given to sleeping, eating, exercise, relaxation, hobbies and holidays.

These costs need to be carefully considered because it is so important that you are aware of them and know how to keep them under control by the use of coping strategies. One of the most important of these is effective time management. A teacher in one of my workshops strongly argued that 'the control of time is crucial to a teacher's wellbeing' and he asked: 'Can teachers be helped towards a more effective and therefore satisfying use of time?' I agree with him about the importance of time management because of the following benefits and equally strongly I believe that the answer to his question is 'Yes'.

Ten benefits of successful time management

1 More effective stress management
2 Clearer thinking
3 Better forward planning
4 More time available for more important tasks
5 Better personal relationships
6 Better use of information
7 Greater self-confidence and credibility
8 Better quality work
9 More work done
10 Improvement of career prospects.

To achieve these benefits, here are some practical suggestions to help you to organize your own personal work and the way you spend your time more effectively. Check yourself against this six-point programme once a month for the next six months. The programme is based on one proposed by John Adair in his book *Effective Leadership* (1983).

1 Develop a new personal sense of time. Do not rely on memory. Record where your time goes.
2 Plan ahead. Make plans on how you are going to spend your time each day, week, month, term and year. Plan in respect of opportunities and results, priorities and deadlines.
3 Make the most of your best time. Programme important tasks for the time of day you function best. Have planned quiet periods for creative thinking.
4 Avoid clutter. Sort papers into categories according to action priorities. Generate as little paper as possible yourself.
5 Do it now. 'Procrastination is the thief of time.'
6 Learn to say 'No'. Do not let others misappropriate your time. Decline tactfully but firmly to avoid over-commitment.

The first of these six suggestions can be achieved by the use of a framework to enable you to record where your time is being spent. A time log can be used for this purpose. If the analysis of the log indicates that time spent at school or at home on school work dominates your time profile almost to the exclusion of other non-work activities you may decide (I hope) that you need to improve your time-management skills. Adair's suggestions are helpful, but I would like to add two more:

7 Identify your main sources of time loss and block up the holes! These may be from the many different kinds of interruptions which teachers experience. They may be from children, parents, colleagues, the head, or outside agencies, and firm action is required to prevent time loss, or time theft, as I would prefer to call it, becoming a significant problem.
8 Objectively consider if the meetings you attend in school are a major source of time theft. If the robber is the head because of his or her poor management of meetings some discussion of the following seven suggestions at your next staff meeting can be the starting point for this particular improvement.

Effective meetings

1 Have as few as possible.
2 Calendar in advance.
3 Restrict agenda to a few items.
4 Be clear about purpose of agenda – are items for discussion, recommendation or decision?
5 Circulate agenda and minutes at least a week in advance.
6 Start and end meetings at the time announced.
7 Act on decisions rapidly.

Guidelines for assertiveness

The above suggestions possibly mean that another skill has to be developed: the skill of assertiveness. Being assertive is not the same as being aggressive. The differences between assertive behaviour, aggressive behaviour and passive behaviour are:

Assertive behaviour – enables people to act in their own best interests and stand up for their rights, whilst also respecting the rights and feelings of others. It enables people to express both positive and negative feeling comfortably and without undue anxiety.

Aggressive behaviour – involves people trying to get what they want, at all costs, with no regard for the feelings of others, by bullying, sarcasm, threatening or putting down other people. It can also involve less direct aggression – using manipulative and devious means like emotional blackmail and flattery.

Passive behaviour – involves the denial of personal feelings and rights which are rarely expressed openly. Needs are therefore seldom met – with a consequent loss of self-esteem. Typical behaviours are sighing, hinting, wishing and sulking.

Typical situations in school in which assertiveness is valuable are when a teacher is blamed for a mistake for which he or she is not responsible, or when a member of staff is asked to undertake a new area of work despite being already over-burdened or when a teacher is asked to finish a project within an unrealistic deadline.

Saying 'No' to these demands is often regarded as unprofessional and the person who manages to do it often feels guilty; but if you want to halt the severe loss of your time please practise this lovely word. You will then have more time available for the job and more available for planning and implementing the National Curriculum. You will also have the time, energy and assertive skills to monitor and to tackle effectively other important changes and challenges to your role which in my view are being exacerbated by the Education Reform Act. These include a challenge to your professional status and autonomy from the National Curriculum, but particularly from LMS.

The reports of the working parties were compiled into 'A Report on Managing College Stress – In-Service Training', in which it was stated: 'The findings of the groups will form the basis for future discussions'. Time management was identified as a major concern by many members of staff and this interest was reflected in the large number of reports on this problem. I want to include the reports of two groups to illustrate the 'whole-school' approach of the college to stress-management training.

Time Management: report on the meeting of the administrative staff

The discussion started with some frank comments on how the office staff frequently felt that they were regarded as 'second-class citizens' as far as the staffing of the college was concerned. It was felt that we were expected to do too many jobs at the same time. We are expected to keep all equipment running smoothly, whether we use it or not; we are expected to stop what we are doing to attend to someone's needs even though we are undertaking (mostly without training) new tasks for LMS.

The office staff see themselves as an integral part of the college and consider that they have three main roles:
(a) As a working department.

(b) As a support to the rest of the staff.

(c) As the first contact point in the college, responsible for receiving visitors and projecting a good image.

They believe that they have a role to play in the time management of the teaching staff. It was generally considered that, although the office staff are very aware of the changes which are taking place in the teaching profession, it was doubtful whether the teaching profession was aware of all the changes which administrative staff are having to take on board.

The following recommendations were made:

1 Non-teaching staff should have equal status with teaching staff.
2 Staff meetings should be attended by all categories of staff.
3 There should be better liaison between staff.
4 The office should give a presentation of available services; it was felt that sometimes we were abused rather than used.
5 Teaching staff should recognize the space and time belonging to administrative staff.
6 Administrative deadlines should be met.
7 There should be a Development Plan for support staff.
8 Training should be given in the new technology and assertiveness.
9 There should be INSET for support staff.

Time management: report on the meeting of technicians

The following recommendations were made:

1 Time should be available for technicians to meet.
2 There should be opportunities for technicians and support staff to give presentations.
3 Needs should be anticipated by careful pre-planning.
4 There should be an opportunity to attend staff meetings.
5 There should be a development programme for support staff.
6 There should be a recognition of personal time/space by others.
7 There should be more consultative time.
8 There should be more opportunities for consultation with members of Executive.

The report on managing college stress was presented to each member of staff at the beginning of the next term, but I had received the first feedback in the first week of the summer holiday:

Many thanks for such an excellent day yesterday. The response of the whole staff was very enthusiastic and positive and I really feel that we have begun to look seriously at ways of reducing stress in College. I will keep you in touch with our progress next term.

Progress was reviewed six months later. The INSET co-ordinator in his review to me said: 'The College has made a small beginning towards reducing stress for staff.' He indicated what had already started:

1 Office staff and technicians have access to all meetings in College.
2 A non-teaching and teaching staff support group was started in November. It meets weekly. The facilitator is the INSET co-ordinator. It acts as a forum for the identification of new pressures on staff.
3 There is an effective channel of communication with the Executive as the INSET co-ordinator is invited to its meetings. He believes that the Executive has tried very hard to respond to the demands from the support group. He has also presented a report on stress management to the College Board.
4 A year plan has been placed on the college wall providing information about important dates, deadlines and activities. This strategy is enabling staff to identify likely pressure points and 'to change things in advance'.
5 Steps have been taken to reduce role conflict by improving role definition. The management structure in the college has been redrafted to clarify all roles and areas of responsibility – including the kitchen staff. The role conflict between the pastoral (set) tutor role and the subject tutor role is the present focus of concern for the Support Group and the Executive. Their attempt at conflict resolution is directed specifically at the set tutor period. This was identified by me as a major pressure for some staff and it has been reported to the Support Group because 'staff are still pressurizing each other' as there are strongly expressed differences of opinion about its purpose.

This review of stress-management strategies suggests that an effective means of reducing teacher stress 'is to encourage teachers themselves to assume responsibility for the identification of stressors and planning appropriate staff development programmes on coping techniques' (Tollan 1990:110). My recommended whole-school model of stress management seeks to open up pathways of support in all directions in an organization – upwards, sideways and downwards. It encourages the sharing of resources between all members of the school community – teachers, non-teaching staff, pupils and governors. It proposes an active policy of participation by all members in the continuing development of a school as a healthy organization in the 1990s.

An excellent guide for the whole-school management programmes which staff will need in the 1990s to deliver and sustain all the reforms of the 1988 Act has been prepared by the Education Service Advisory Committee of the Health and Safety Commission and published by HMSO (1990). Their recommended strategies have been presented in the form of a checklist:

Managing Stress

- Develop a supportive culture.
- Are you countering the view that stress is a reflection of personal vulnerability?
- Are senior managers accessible to staff to discuss problems?
- Are staff encouraged to support colleagues and to talk about feelings and effects of stress?
- Is the management style co-operative rather than competitive?
- How is team spirit, a sense of belonging and sharing of aims and objectives encouraged?
- Are induction and introduction programmes for new staff effective?
- Do you recognize individuals' fears about returning to work after sickness?
- Do staff make use of occupational health advice?
- Do you encourage group problem-solving?
- Do you emphasize prevention and preparing rather than coping with stress?
- Have staff discussed whole school policies and action plans designed to reduce stress arising from:
  discipline and disruptive pupils
  training, induction and career development
  workload
  lack of resources
  the state of the school
  staff facilities
  school organization
  communications
  political and community expectations.

(Harrison 1990:23)

These guidelines provide an essential monitoring framework for schools to use as they become more effective in stress management. Within this broad framework each school should have its own programme and objectives formulated by staff after a stress audit, which could be organized by one or more colleagues as my students have demonstrated in this chapter. Following one such audit one student made the following policy recommendations to her colleagues:

It is important that staff feel they are part of a caring environment. Thus it is important to show that staff are recognized as individuals by:

- Acknowledging their successes (e.g. mention in school magazine if member of staff achieved M.Ed.).
- Noticing staff absence (e.g. organizing cards and gifts to staff who are ill and showing genuine interest and concern on their return).
- Remembering staff have a life outside school (e.g. notices about outside activities – theatre, sports clubs) and ought to be encouraged to do activities where they can switch off.
- Giving perks to staff (e.g. free school lunch for attendance at meetings).
- Encouraging socializing amongst staff and managers (e.g. organizing social events – skittles, car treasure hunts). If such activities are organized by the staff social committee it is important that staff at all levels attend, as one of the major concerns by staff is the lack of social contact with an SMT and an 'us and them' syndrome developing.
- Staff felt that there should be some kind of support system to alleviate their stress. They wanted to be able to talk to staff who were approachable and available and made them feel appreciated. Within the school the new female deputy head commented during our fortnightly meetings that there was a definite need, as since her arrival a large number of staff had come into her office for a 'good cry'. Some form of support system would provide a forum to be frank. However the success of such a scheme depends on confidentiality, or staff would always fear what they were saying would be written down and held against them – that they were being judged and not supported. Thus such a system would to a large extent have to be informal and perhaps link staff with those of a similar position (i.e. assistant head of year to be supported by another) so they can appreciate their fears and moans.

These policy recommendations for a caring environment provide a fine conclusion to this chapter and to my book. I end it with my best wishes for the success of your stress-reduction programmes.

APPENDIX

Teachers' reactions to industrial action

What are your colleagues' reactions to industrial action? What are yours? From teachers' replies to these questions I have noted the following positive and negative statements. Please identify by (√) your reactions:

1 My reactions are positive because unnecessary meetings are a thing of the past ( )
2 Mine are positive because there are no pressures to have meetings after school ( )
3 Mine are negative because of the conflict between those teachers who have acted and those who have not ( )
4 My feelings are negative because new teachers and students on TP will take the current situation to be the norm ( )
5 My reactions are negative because older pupils resent the absence of those things they enjoyed like sport, clubs, activities ( )
6 Mine are positive because of opportunities of relaxation at lunchtime ( )
7 Mine are negative because industrial action has increased the pressures on the head ( )
8 I am frustrated by industrial action because very little is happening within the department ( )
9 I am frustrated because I think that relationships and communication with parents will not be re-established for a long time ( )
10 I am worried because I do not know how to cope with the disillusioned members of my team who do not wish to return to doing voluntary duties when the action ends ( )
11 My reactions are negative because staff relationships which were formerly good are becoming strained as a result of different union loyalties ( )
12 My reactions are negative because of my colleagues' growing disillusionment with the job e.g. two departmental heads are leaving teaching without having a job to go to ( )

13 Mine are negative because industrial action might kill extra-curricular activities ( )

14 Mine are positive because of guaranteed 'non-teaching' time for preparation, marking or even relaxing! ( )

15 My feelings are negative because the parents and children in my school seem to be developing the idea that teachers are a non-caring group ( )

16 Industrial action has brought the negative result of a lessening of communication between management and staff e.g. now only by printed messages ( )

17 I am worried that management from the top 'by dictat' will become the norm ( )

18 I am worried by possible 'parental negativity' to the action taken by staff ( )

19 Industrial action has meant for me the release of many pressures ( )

20 There is a release of the feeling that if you didn't go to meetings it would affect your reference/career ( )

21 My frustration comes at the hierarchy's response to the unpopular decisions they make: they say 'No meetings are possible' ( )

22 My feelings about industrial action are negative because vandalism and bad behaviour have increased ( )

23 Leaving school at lunchtime does provide a pleasant break from the routine of school ( )

24 I feel that I have been unable to provide the advice/guidance which is normally available to pupils re their careers ( )

25 I have yet to note a single benefit from industrial action and feel extremely frustrated, over-stressed and look forward to early retirement a.s.a.p. ( )

26 I am exhausted by trying to retain standards without the assistance of other colleagues ( )

BIBLIOGRAPHY

Abrams, F. (1990) 'Teachers "desert schools in record numbers" ', *Sunday Times*, 6 May: A4.

Adair, J. (1983) *Effective Leadership*, London: Pan.

Albrecht, K. (1979) *Stress and the Manager*, Englewood Cliffs, N. J.: Prentice-Hall.

Appley, M. H. (1967) Invited commentary in Appley, M. H. and Trumbull, R. (eds) *Psychological Stress*, New York: Appleton Century Crofts.

Appley, M. H. and Trumbull, R. (1967) (eds) *Psychological Stress*, New York: Appleton Century Crofts.

Armes, D. (1985) *The Unhappiest 'Profession'*, Bradford: Armes.

Back, K. and Back, K. (1982) *Assertiveness at Work*, London: Guild Publishing.

Barrell, G. (1983) 'Knowing the law' in A. Paisley (ed.) *The Effective Teacher*, London: Ward Lock Educational.

Bell, L. and Maher, P. (1986) *Leading a Pastoral Team*, Oxford: Blackwell.

Bispham, G. R. (1980) *Initial Report on Antisocial Behaviour in Schools*, Northamptonshire County Council.

Blackburn, K. (1983) 'The pastoral head: a developing role', *Pastoral Care in Education*, 1: 18–24.

Blackie, P. (1977) 'Not quite proper', *Times Educational Supplement*, 25 November: 20–1.

Blase, J. J. (1982) 'A social-psychological grounded theory of teacher stress and burnout', *Educational Administration Quarterly* 18, 4: 93–113.

Bone, T. (1983) 'Exercising leadership' in A. Paisey (ed.) *The Effective Teacher*, London: Ward Lock Educational.

Brown, G. W. and Harris, T. (1978) *Social Origins of Depression*, London: Tavistock.

Burke, E. and Dunham, J. (1982) 'Identifying stress in language teaching', *British Journal of Language Teaching* 20: 149–52.

Buss, A. H. (1961) *The Psychology of Aggression*, New York: Wiley.

Butler-Sloss, E. (1988) *Report of the Inquiry into Child Abuse in Cleveland 1987*, London: HMSO.

Campbell, R. J. and Neill, S. St J. (1990) *Teacher Time in Key Stage 1: Thirteen Hundred and Thirty Days*, London: Assistant Masters and Mistresses Association.

Caplan, G. (1964) *Principles of Preventive Psychiatry*, New York: Basic Books.

Casey, T. (1976) Introduction to *Stress in Schools*, Hemel Hempstead: NAS/UWT.

Charlton, T. and David, K. (1989) (eds) *Managing Misbehaviour*, London: Macmillan.

Cherniss, G. (1980) *Professional Burnout in Human Service Organisations*, New York: Praeger.

Chisholm, B., Kearney, T., Knight, M., Little, C., Morris, B., and Tweddle, A. (1986) *Preventive Approaches to Disruption (PAD)*, London: Macmillan Education.

Claxton, G. (1989) *Being a Teacher: A Positive Approach to Change, Innovation and Stress*, London: Cassell.

Clwyd County Council (1976) *Absenteeism and Disruptive Behaviour*, Mold: Clwyd County Council.

Cotgrove, S. F., Dunham, J., and Vamplew, C. (1971) *The Nylon Spinners*, London: Allen & Unwin.

Courtis, J. (1988) *Interviews: Skills and Strategies*, London: Institute of Personnel Management.

Cowan, B. J. and Wright, N. (1988) '1265: An examination of some of the management implications of directed time', *School Organisation* 8, 3: 301–14.

—— (1989) 'Directed time, a year on: staff perspectives', *School Organisation* 9, 3: 375–89.

Critchley, B. and Casey, D. (1986) 'Managing effective teams' in Mumford, A. (ed.) *Handbook of Management Development*, Aldershot: Gower.

Department of Education and Science (1985) *Better Schools*, London: HMSO.

—— (1989) *National Curriculum from Policy to Practice*, London: Department of Education and Science.

—— (1989) *School Teacher Appraisal: A National Framework. Report of the National Steering Group on the School Teacher Appraisal Pilot Study*, London: Department of Education and Science.

Department of Education and Science and Welsh Office (1989) *Discipline in Schools (Elton Report)*, London: HMSO.

Dunham, J. (1976a) 'Stress situations and responses' in *Stress in Schools*, Hemel Hempstead: NAS/UWT.

—— (1976b) 'The Reduction of Stress' in *Stress in Schools*, Hemel Hempstead: NAS/UWT.

—— (1978) 'Change and Stress in the Head of Department's Role', *Educational Research*, 21, 44–7.

—— (1980a) 'An exploratory comparative study of staff stress in English and German comprehensive schools', *Educational Review* 32, 11–20.

—— (1980b) 'The effects of communication difficulties on social workers', *Social Work Today* 11: 10–12.

—— (1981a) 'Resources checklist to help you reduce tension at work', *Social Work Today*, 12: 29.

—— (1981b) 'Disruptive pupils and teacher stress', *Educational Research* 23: 3, 205–13.

—— (1982) 'Stress in Schools', *Times Educational Supplement*, 23 July: 18–20.

—— (1986) *Stress in Teaching*, London: Routledge.

—— (1987) 'Caring for the Pastoral Carers', *Pastoral Care in Education* 5, 1: 15–21.

Earley, P. and Fletcher-Campbell, F. (1989) *The Time to Manage?* London: NFER-Nelson.

Earley, P., Baker, L. and Weindling, R. (1990) *Keeping the Raft Afloat: Secondary Headship Five Years On*, Slough: NFER-Nelson.

Education Service Advisory Committee of the Health and Safety Commission (1990) *Managing Occupational Stress: A Guide for Managers and Teachers in the School Sector*, London: HMSO.

Everard, K. B. and Morris, G. (1985) *Effective School Management*, London: Harper & Row.

Eysenck, H. J. (1975) *Encyclopedia of Psychology II*, London: Fontana/Collins.

Farley, R. (1989) *Your Discipline in School*, London: New Education Press.

Finch, R. (1990) 'New pressures on heads', *Times Educational Supplement* 16 March: 27.

Fontana, D. (1989) *Managing Stress*, London: Routledge.

Forney, D. S., Wallace-Schutzman, F. and Wiggers, T. (1982) 'Burnout among career development professionals: Preliminary findings and implications', *Personnel and Guidance Journal*, March: 435–9.

Friedman, M. and Rosenman, R. (1974) *Type A Behaviour and Your Heart*, Fawcett, Conn.: Greenwich Publications.

Friedman, M. and Ulmer, D. (1985) *Treating Type A Behaviour and Your Heart*, London: Guild Publishing.

Galloway, D. (1987) 'Disruptive behaviour in school', *Educational and Child Psychology* 4, 1: 29–34.

Galloway, D., Ball, T., Blomfield, D. and Seyd, R. (1982) *Schools and Disruptive Pupils*, London: Longman.

Galloway, D. and Goodwin, C. (1987) *The Education of Disturbing Children*, London: Longman.

Gammage, P. (1988) Letter to *The Psychologist* 1, 11: 437.

Gardell, D. (1971) 'Alienation and Mental Health in the Modern Industrial Environment' in L. Levi (ed.) *Society, Stress and Disease*, Oxford: Oxford University Press.

Gow, F. (1989) 'Governors' new powers', *Guardian*, 24 June: 6.

Grice, C. and Hanke, M. (1990) 'Suspending judgements: teacher appraisal', *Education Today* 40, 2: 42–4.

Hall, T. W. (1990) 'In need of a full stop', *Times Educational Supplement*, 20 July: 19.

Hanko, G. (1989) 'After Elton – how to manage disruption', *British Journal of Special Education* 16, 4: 140–3.

Harrison, P. (1990) 'Tackling the high cost of stress', *Times Educational Supplement* 28 December.

Health Promotion Research Trust (1989) *Less Stress More Success*, Cambridge: Health Promotion Research Trust.

Health and Safety Commission (1990) *Managing Occupational Stress: A Guide for Managers and Teachers in the Schools Sector*, London: HMSO.

Hebb, D. (1972) *Textbook of Psychology*, Philadelphia: Saunders.

Hilsum, S. and Cane, P. (1971) *The Teacher's Day*, Slough: NFER.

Hinton, M. G. (1974) 'Teaching in large schools', *Headmasters Association Review* LXXII, 220: 17–19.

Houghton, S., Wheldall, K. and Merrett, F. (1988) 'Classroom behaviour which secondary school teachers say they find most troublesome' *British Educational Research Journal* 14, 3: 297–312.

Hoyle, E. (1969) *The Role of the Teacher*, London: Routledge & Kegan Paul.

Humberside Federation of NAS/UWT (1991) *Stress Report*, Spring.

Humphrey, P. T. (1983) 'Recruitment and selection' in D. Lock and N. Farrow (eds) *The Gower Book of Management*, Aldershot: Gower.

Janis, I. (1971) *Stress and Frustration*, New York: Harcourt Brace Jovanovich.

Janner, G. (1989) *Guide to Employment and Industrial Relations Law for Headteachers*, London: National Association of Headteachers.

Jay, A. (1976) *How to Run a Meeting*, London: Video Arts.

Jenkins, H. O. (1989) 'Educational managers – paradigms lost', *Studies in Educational Administration* 51: 3–27.

John, D. (1972) 'Going comprehensive: staff roles and relationships as factors in innovation', *Forum* 15, 1: 7–9.

Johnston, D. W. (1989) 'Will stress management prevent coronary heart disease?' *Psychological Bulletin* 7: 275–8.

Jones, N. (ed.) (1989) *Special Educational Needs: Review 1*, Lewes: The Falmer Press.

Kahn, R. L. (1973) 'Conflict, ambiguity and overload: three elements in job stress', *Occupational Mental Health* 3, 1: 191–4.

Kahn, R. L., Wolfe, D. M., Quinn, R. P., Snock, J. D. and Rosenthal, R. A. (1964) *Organisational Stress*, New York: Wiley.

Knewstub, P. (1990) 'Local management of schools', *Guardian*, 28 March, 6.

Knutton, K. and Mycroft, A. (1986) 'Stress and the deputy head', *School Organisation* 6, 1: 49–59.

Kruger, C., Summers, M. and Palacio, D. (1990) 'Mixed reactions', *Times Educational Supplement*, 30 March: 20.

Kyriacou, C. (1980) 'Coping action and organisational stress among school teachers', *Research in Education* 24, 57–61.

—— (1981) 'Social support and occupational stress among school teachers', *Educational Studies* 7, 1: 55–60.

Lambert, K. (1986) *School Management*, Oxford: Blackwell.

Lancashire County Council (1980) *Active Tutorial Work*, Oxford: Blackwell.

Lawrence, J., Steed, D. and Young, P. (1983) 'Monitoring teachers' reports of incidents of disruptive behaviour in two secondary schools: multidisciplinary research and intervention', *Educational Studies* 9, 2: 141–53.

Lazarus, R. (1981) 'Little hassles can be hazardous to health', *Psychology Today* July: 58–62.

Levi, L. (1971) (ed.) *Society, Stress and Disease I*, Oxford: Oxford University Press.

Livingstone-Booth, A. (1985) *Stressmanship*, London: Severn House.

Luke, A. C. (1980) 'Communication in education: a case-study of the headteacher's role in the primary school', unpublished M.Ed. thesis, University of Cardiff School of Education.

McMahon, A. (1989) 'School teacher appraisal schemes in England: the pilot scheme experience in Wilson, J. D. *et al.*, *Assessment for Teacher Development*, London: Falmer.

McManus, M. (1989) *Troublesome Behaviour in the Classroom*, London: Routledge.

Manning, M. R., Williams, R. F. and Wolfe, D. M. (1988) 'Hardiness and the relationship between stressors and outcomes', *Work and Stress* 2, 3: 205–16.

Marland, M. (1971) *Head of Department*, London: Heinemann.

—— (1983) 'Preparing for promotion in pastoral care', *Pastoral Care in Education* 1, 1: 24–35.

Marland, M. and Hill, S. (1981) *Departmental Management*, London: Heinemann.

Masidlover, L. (1981) 'Simple nine-point plan to beat stress', *National Enquirer*, July: 53.

Mechanic, D. (1967) Invited commentary in K. H. Appley and R. Trumbull (eds) *Psychological Stress*, New York: Appleton Century Crofts.

Meichenbaum, D. H. (1975) 'A self-instructional approach to stress management: a proposal for stress inoculation training' in C. D. Spielberger and I. G. Sarason (eds) *Stress and Anxiety I*, New York: Hemisphere Publishing Company.

Mongon, D. and Hart, S. with Ace, C. and Rawlings, A. (1989) *Improving Classroom Behaviour: New Directions for Teachers and Pupils*, London: Cassell.

Monro, R. (1985) 'Progress of yoga survey' *Yoga Today*: July: 34.

Morant, R. (1983) 'Developing a personal career' in A. Paisley (ed.) *The Effective Teacher*, London: Ward Lock Educational.

Morgan, C. (1983) *Selection of Heads*, Milton Keynes: Open University.

Mumford, A. (1986) (ed.) *Handbook of Management Development*, Aldershot: Gower.

Murgatroyd, S. and Woolfe, R. (1982) *Coping with Crisis*, London: Harper & Row.

National Steering Group (1989) *A National Framework Report, School Appraisal*, London: HMSO.

Northamptonshire LEA (n.d.) *Staff Development Programme for Northamptonshire Schools*, Northamptonshire LEA.

Open University E321–14 (1976) *Role of the educational manager and the individual in the organisation*, Milton Keynes: Open University Press.

Paisey, A. (1983) (ed.) *The Effective Teacher*, London: Ward Lock Educational.

Parkes, K. R. (1988) 'Stress, coping and the work environment', paper given at the British Psychological Society meeting, London, December.

Pines, A. and Maslach, C. (1978) 'Characteristics of staff burnout in mental health settings', *Hospital and Community Psychiatry* 29: 233–7.

Plant, R. (1987) *Managing Change and Making it Stick*, London: Fontana/Collins.

Polumin, M. (1980) *The Health and Fitness Handbook*, New York: Frances Lincoln/ Windward.

Pratt, K. J. and Steyning, R. J. (1989) *Managing Staff Appraisal in Schools*, London: Van Nostrand Reinhold.

Raab, W. (1971) 'Preventive Myocardiology – Proposals for Social Action' in L. Levi (ed.) *Society, Stress and Disease* I, Oxford: Oxford University Press.

Redman, S., Brerton, A. and Boyers, P. (1969) *An Approach to Primary Science: Oxford Primary Science Project*, London: Macmillan.

Richardson, E. (1973) *The Teacher, the School and the Task of Management*, London: Tavistock.

Rudge, P. F. (1976) *Ministry and Management*, London: Tavistock.

Selye, H. (1956) *The Stress of Life*, New York: McGraw-Hill.

Shaw, H. (1986) 'A burnout case', *Times Educational Supplement*, 31 January.

Silva, J. and Mieli P. (1977) *The Silva Mind Control Method*, New York: Simon & Schuster.

Simpson, T. (1987) 'Headteacher stress', *School Organisation* 7, 3: 281–5.

Simpson, J. (1974) 'The times they are a failing', *Guardian*, 21 May: 5.

Skynner, A. C. R. (1975) 'An experiment in group consultation with the staff of a comprehensive school', *Group Process* 66: 99–114.

Smithers, A. and Robinson, P. (1990) *Teacher Loss*, Manchester University School of Education.

Styan, D. (1989) 'Don't panic', *Times Educational Supplement*, 27 January: 29.

Sutcliffe, J. (1989) 'Warming to the idea of cold selling', *Times Educational Supplement*, 16 June: A5.

Symonds, G. P. (1947) 'Use and abuse of the term flying stress', in Air Ministry (1947) *Psychological disorders in flying personnel of the Royal Air Force, investigated during the War 1939–1945*.

Thompson, P. (1987) *School Self-Evaluation*, Scarborough Teachers Publishing Group.

Thompson, Q. (1990) 'Is LMS still on track?, *Times Educational Supplement*, 6 July: 14.

Thoreson, C. E., Telch, M. J. and Engleston, J. R. (1981) 'Approaches to altering the Type A behaviour pattern', *Psychosomatics* 22, 6: 472–82.

Tollan, J. (1990) 'Stress-aid: A whole-school approach to stress prevention', unpublished M.Sc. thesis, University of Stirling.

Travers, C. and Cooper, C. (1990) *Survey on occupational stress among teachers in the United Kingdom*, Manchester: University of Manchester Institute of Science and Technology.

Vaughan, C. (1990) 'Unbalanced laughter', *Guardian*, 27 March: 19.

Warwick, D. (1983) *Staff Appraisal*, London: The Industrial Society Press.

Watson, D. (1986) 'Cost benefit analysis' *School Organisation* 16, January–April.

Weeks, A. (1989) *Your Local Management of Schools*, London: New Education Press.

Wilson, J. D., Thomson, G. O. B., Millward, R. E. and Keenan, T. (eds) (1989) *Assessment for Teacher Development*, Brighton: Falmer.

Wiltshire County Council Education Department (1981) *Deputy Headship – Guidelines for Good Practice*, Trowbridge: Wiltshire County Council.

Witkin-Lanoil, G. (1985) *Coping with Stress*, London: Sheldon Press.

Woolcott, L. (1983) 'Achieving administrative efficiency' in A. Paisey (ed.) *The Effective Teacher*, London: Ward Lock Educational.

Wragg, T. (1990) 'Out of the Wood – National Curriculum update', *Times Educational Supplement*, 20 July: 20.

INDEX